Marriage Medicine

Character *is the* Cure

TYRONE HOLCOMB

CREATION
HOUSE

MARRIAGE MEDICINE: CHARACTER IS THE CURE
by Tyrone Holcomb
Published by Creation House
A Charisma Media Company
600 Rinehart Road
Lake Mary, Florida 32746
www.charismamedia.com

Unless otherwise noted, all Scripture quotations are from the Holy Bible, New Century Version. Copyright © 1987, 1988, 1991 by Word Publishing, Dallas, Texas 75039. Used by permission.

Scripture quotations marked AMP are from the Amplified Bible. Old Testament copyright © 1965, 1987 by the Zondervan Corporation. The Amplified New Testament copyright © 1954, 1958, 1987 by the Lockman Foundation. Used by permission.

Scripture quotations marked KJV are from the King James Version of the Bible.

Scripture quotations marked THE MESSAGE are from *The Message: The Bible in Contemporary English*, copyright © 1993, 1994, 1995, 1996, 2000, 2001, 2002. Used by permission of NavPress Publishing Group.

Scripture quotations marked NIV are from the Holy Bible, New International Version. Copyright © 1973, 1978, 1984, 2010, 2011, International Bible Society. Used by permission.

Scripture quotations marked NLT are from the Holy Bible, New Living Translation, copyright © 1996. Used by permission of Tyndale House Publishers, Inc., Wheaton, IL 60189. All rights reserved.

English definitions are derived from *Webster's Third New International Dictionary Unabridged* (Springfield, MA: Merriam-Webster's, 2002).

Design Director: Bill Johnson
Cover design by Terry Clifton

Visit the author's website: www.chop.org

Library of Congress Cataloging-in-Publication Data: 2012946652
International Standard Book Number: 978-1-62136-101-5
E-book International Standard Book Number: 978-1-62136-306-4

While the author has made every effort to provide accurate telephone numbers and Internet addresses at the time of publication, neither the publisher nor the author assumes any responsibility for errors or for changes that occur after publication.

First edition

12 13 14 15 16 — 9 8 7 6 5 4 3 2 1
Printed in Canada

So don't lose a minute in building on what you've been given, complementing your basic faith with good character, spiritual understanding, alert discipline, passionate patience, reverent wonder, warm friendliness, and generous love, each dimension fitting into and developing the others. With these qualities active and growing in your lives, no grass will grow under your feet, no day will pass without its reward as you mature in your experience of our Master Jesus.

—2 Peter 1:5–8, The Message

Acknowledgments

You, the reader—I am elated you are reading this book. I pray these pages will challenge you to become a better person. In turn, may you positively affect the lives of others.

Those I've counseled—thank you for allowing me to speak into your lives. Stay connected to the Vine (Jesus) and your marriage/life will continue bearing fruit.

The Covenant Connections International Family—many of you allowed me into your pulpits to teach the truths of this book. For your love and support I am grateful.

The Christian House of Prayer Family—it was your ardent desire and prayers to see this work completed which allowed me to succeed. I am fortunate to serve as one of your Elders and to be your brother in Christ.

Ramona Johnson—a threefold cord is not easily broken (you, me, and, of course, the Holy Spirit). I enjoyed editing this book together. It's the only time I really get to laugh at myself, and you never mind joining in. Thanks for all you do, you're the best!

My mother—your love and support serves as wind beneath my wings. Love you unconditionally!

My father—it is one of my life's goals to make you as proud of me as I am of you. I pray this book brings me closer to that desire. I am honored and humbled to serve with you in the ministry.

My children—I will always have four reasons to do my very best and they are Omar, Vaughn, Jada, and Ty. With passion and purpose, I love you all.

My wife—my life is enriched with colors and sounds all because you are around. See—you still bring out the poet in me (smile). In you I've found the perfect lover and friend. I more than love you; I like you!

My Lord—I truly thank You for Your time, Your touch, and our talks. As I surrender myself, I desire my life to yield fruit to the glory of Your Name. Without You I can do nothing; with You all things are possible!

Contents

Foreword

In a world where the union of marriage is both attacked and abandoned, I am both excited and elated about the authoring and release of the book *Marriage Medicine*. In it Tyrone has captured the very heart of our heavenly Father and unlocked the source of true health and healing for hurting relationships.

I have known this man of God for nearly twenty years. Of all the books and poems authored by him, this is by far the most impacting and in-depth.

Marriage Medicine speaks to the core of conflicts experienced by couples and shows a roadmap out of those crushing confrontations lived on a day-to-day basis. From the beginning of the book, it is clear each chapter is pregnant with the ability to cause progress in the problem areas faced in marriages today.

Tyrone Holcomb has an incredible God-given ability to place truth alongside natural and humorous illustrations to show things always known but rarely revealed. His gift of expression through writing is one of the greatest that I have seen in any man. The insight and wisdom shared in these pages is remarkable; and it is undeniable that this is God's special assignment on his life.

After pastoring for several years and spending countless hours of counseling with married couples, I've discovered that medicine for the modern day marriage is exactly what this generation needs. Having seen and read many books and materials on this subject, I have found this one to be very practical, powerful, and also profound. I am confident you will find it one of the greatest collections of truths and answers released to date.

It is obvious the authoring of this book has been ordained by God and given the special task of bringing not only deliverance but also development to what has devastated marriages for years.

I hear the Word of the Lord declaring, "*Marriage Medicine* will be a remedy and resource used by countless people for years and years to come." Romans 8:19 tells us that the whole earth is waiting for the manifestation of the sons of God. Likewise marriages around the world have been waiting to discover the life-changing truths unveiled in the pages of this book. Today I too anxiously await and want the world to discover it!

—PASTOR JESSE GIDDENS
DESTINY CHRISTIAN CENTER
VICTORVILLE, CALIFORNIA

Introduction

Many people believe maturity comes automatically with growing *old*. However, this is not necessarily true. Maturity comes with growing *up*. By God's grace, growing old is inevitable; growing up is optional. Therefore, the goal is to grow up.

We can grow old with absolutely no effort. But growing up takes work. So then the question becomes, how do we grow up? Allow me to offer this solution: growing up involves character development. Now there's a word we don't hear enough: *character*.

Character is treated as an antiquated concept that has lost its place. More value is given to academics, athletics, and entertainment than to character. Our society fosters the concept that "what you possess is more important than who you are." As a result of this thinking, our relationships suffer and many people are more concerned with pleasures, positions, and possessions of life rather than possessing the character of Christ.

There's nothing wrong with possessing possessions, but going after materials is fleeting without morals. A person's skill can get them certified, but it's their character which keeps them satisfied. Character keeps us morally sound. Good relationships start with becoming good people.

Problems with our morality often present problems in our reality. Morality deals with right and wrong; reality deals with true and false. Consequently, when a person compromises their morals, sooner or later their perception of what is real is skewed.

Many relationships falter not because there is a lack of love but they fail due to a lack of character. It is my ardent desire to see marriages and all relationships blossom and grow with love and fulfillment. Too many people have to face the harsh reality of ruined relationships. However, this does not have to be the case.

If your relationship is described as mundane or worse, mutinous, the remedy is character. Character causes us to take a deeper look at ourselves. Men spend billions of dollars exploring outer space when the real battle is inner space. Our struggles begin within!

This book was written to provide strategies for the struggle, to give the cure for ailing relationships. And our goal is to take healthy unions to another level of love and strength.

So now I ask you, are you going to settle for growing old or will you seek growing up? By choosing the latter you are confirming this book is just what you've been waiting for.

My prayer is that it will provoke you to reach further, dig deeper, and become better. If your relationship is ill or you desire to make a good relationship better, character is the cure.

COMMITMENT

It is our decisions that create the path we
take in life.

Playing for Keeps

COMMITMENT

Chapter One

I recall the very first time I went fishing on a boat. I was with an older more experienced angler. He and I hit the lake at two o'clock in the morning. We decided to float and frolic until the fish woke up. Our fun converted quickly to an intense anticipation. With our lines sunk deep into the water, our eyes stared for any indication of fish.

Without warning, I had a bite! I reeled my fish in with both passion and precision. My older colleague urged me on. Judging by the fight on this fish, we predicted a whale. Nothing could top this moment. Nothing else mattered. It seemed the fish and I had existed only for this encounter. When my catch finally emerged from its watery gulf, I discovered my whale was a big mouth bass.

The size of the fish didn't stop me from gloating in my glory. I found conquest in my catch. Then suddenly my fishing partner gave a command that seemed totally absurd. He yelled, "Throw it back in the water!" He explained our purpose was not to keep the fish but to catch and release them.

I was stunned to say the least. The time on the boat, the buying and setting of bait was all to catch and release fish back into the water. I cannot adequately express my disappointment. I was made to contemplate letting go of what I longed after. True, my whale turned out to be a big mouth bass, but it was *my* big mouth bass!

My disappointment that day only pales to what God feels about those who treat marriage in like manner. Many approach marriage with a "catch and release" mentality. Some people design prenuptial contracts before planning the wedding. Oddly enough, some treat marriage like milk. Their marriage begins with an expiration date connected to it.

We should catch our spouse to *keep* and not release them. This goal is accomplished through commitment. Commitment is the first key toward having a healthy marriage. Therefore, becoming a person of commitment is vital. In order to possess the character of commitment, you must make the decision to be committed. Also, you must make the right declarations. Finally, you must mind your devotion.

MAKE THE DECISION

And God said, "So a man will leave his father and mother and be united with his wife, and the two will become one body. So there are not two, but one. God has joined the two together, so no one should separate them."

—MATTHEW 19:5–6

Marriage, like anything, can be a good or bad experience. A good marriage depends on the decision you make. Believe it or not, your marriage will show the effects of what you decide in your mind.

Take for instance my lawn. It was significantly different from my neighbor's. We both moved into our homes around the same time. I chose Bermuda for sod while she selected St. Augustine. I was told by professionals Bermuda was great for the challenges of Texas heat. On the other hand, my neighbor's sod would have to fight an uphill battle under Texas conditions. I pitied my neighbor for her choice of grass.

As it turned out, she was quite the green thumb. Eventually her lawn looked like plush green carpet. My grass had more patches than a seasoned Boy Scout. She began displaying a colorful array of flowers on certain sections of her lawn. My grass bulged about with weeds. Her lawn was fertilized with turf builder. My grass was sanitized with Roundup. Her lawn was manicured. My grass just needed curing.

Finally I asked my neighbor how she was able to keep her lawn so beautiful. After all, I had the grass predicted to do well and she didn't. Her reply was simple and yet profound. She told me she had made the decision in the beginning to do what it took to make her lawn attractive. I never made such a decision. I figured by purchasing the better grass it would take care of itself.

Many make the same mistake in marriage. They marry without deciding to do whatever it takes to keep their marriage successful. It is our decisions that create the path we take in life. No one just stumbles into college, the military, the work force, or any relationship. Wherever we find ourselves, it is a result of our decisions.

Ponder the following observation:

> Watch your thoughts, for they become your words. Choose your words, for they become actions. Understand your actions, for they become habits. Study your habits, for they become your character. Develop your character, for it becomes your destiny.
>
> —Pastor John Hagee[1]

Do you want to reach your desired destiny? Well, it begins with you making the right decision. The right decision is to become a committed person. The Bible tells us in Matthew 19:6 that no one should separate what God has joined together. God's plan is for you to finish what you started. Therefore, no outside influence or force should be able to overtake the couple's bond for each other.

A poor man was livid when he confronted his wife with the receipt for a $300 dress she purchased. "How could you spend this kind of money?" he questioned.

"I don't know," she cried. "I was standing in the store and decided to try it on. Then it was like the devil was there urging me and saying, 'You look good in that dress, you should buy it.'"

"Well," the man persisted, "you know how to deal with him. Just say, 'Get behind me Satan!'" "I did that!" replied the wife, "but then he said, 'It looks great from back here, too.'"

Once you have made up your mind, it's difficult to be deterred. The problem is many of us don't make up our minds concerning the things that really matter. Once we make the decision to be committed, we must make the right declarations.

Make the Declaration

The power of words is a phenomenon many have not come to understand. Jesus taught that if we believe and not doubt, we will have whatever we say (Mark 11:23). Problems can rise like mountains. However, we can remove any problem by first speaking the right words.

What kind of person do you want to be? Would you like to be one who has what he says or one who says what he has? The first person says what he wants then takes necessary actions to achieve it. The second only talks about his current condition, and if it's unfavorable, does nothing to change it.

The reason some continue to see their problems is because they only speak about the negative circumstances. The Word of God encourages us to speak *to* our problems. (See Romans 8:31.) Declare you are strong and not weak and above all your problems and not crushed beneath them. Proclaim all of your needs are met and you come behind in nothing.

I cannot stress the importance of speaking well. Invariably there will come times when your union will be challenged. Zachariah and Elizabeth had been asking God for a child for quite some time. The times dictated the possibility of Elizabeth being scoffed at and shamed because she had no children.

Finally, God sent His angel with great news that this couple would conceive a child. Strangely enough, upon receiving the news, Zachariah was filled with doubt. Through disbelief, he began questioning the news (Luke 1:18). Therefore, God placed Zachariah's mouth on mute. He was unable to speak until he declared what God declared about his situation (vv. 63–64).

When you are committed to a cause, your words will reveal it, your actions will show it, and others will know it. You don't have to fear for your marriage or your life, not when you learn the power of words.

Consider Abraham. God commanded Abraham to sacrifice his son. Abraham wasn't sure of God's intentions or of the outcome. However, when faced with the arduous task, Abraham made a bold declaration. He told his servants that he and his son would return to them again (Gen. 22:5). Given the task to kill his son, somehow Abraham had faith to declare his son would remain alive. The results of the journey proved Abraham right.

When you are committed, not only do you declare good intentions but you also remember your devotion.

MIND THE DEVOTION

But I made an agreement with my eyes not to look with desire at a girl.

—JOB 31:1

Most marriages begin with a proposal. This can be a time of nervousness and excitement. When proposing the person anxiously awaits the acceptance to the offer of marriage. Excitement fills the air if the reply is favorable.

The proposal is important. Notwithstanding, the promise carries far more weight. The promise connotes the person's commitment to the marriage. The proposal is the offer made; the promise makes the person the offering. In other words, you must promise to be there for your spouse. Nevertheless, you make the promise of commitment to yourself. The previous scripture said Job made an agreement with his eyes. This is to say, he made a promise to himself to be faithful.

Many people begin marriages making promises to their potential mate and even to God concerning their fidelity. However, they never make a promise to themselves to be faithful. A committed person remembers their devotion. Understand that our devotion must first be to God. When we love God first, we'll love our spouse right. If our marriages are to be divorce proof, loving God is both sequential and essential.

One morning Andrea and I were brushing our teeth. With water running and a mouth full of toothpaste, I looked Andrea in her big brown eyes and announced, "I love Jesus more than I love you." Now, I have to admit, I didn't get quite the response I was looking for. I thought Andrea would fall into my arms and shower me with affection. Instead, she gave me a rag to wipe my mouth along with a puzzling stare as if trying to figure out if I was being charming or sarcastic. At the time charm wasn't what I was reaching for, but neither was sarcasm.

Quite frankly, it was as if the lightbulb over my head came on and I realized for the first time that if I am to keep my devotion to Andrea intact, I must love God first and love God final. When you love God first and final, you take on His nature. "God is love" and He lives in those who love others (1 John 4:16).

A proper devotion is to love God first and to love God more. We must love God more than our spouse and more than ourselves. Too often couples are in marriages trying to fulfill their own agendas. In light of this, it becomes paramount for us to see that loving Jesus more only leads to serving our spouse better. In turn, this solidifies our marriage.

Consider the account with Jesus and Peter and study closely how Jesus' inquisition of love was followed with instruction to lead and feed.

> "Simon son of John do you love me *more than these*?" He answered, "Yes, Lord, you know that I love you." Jesus said, "Feed my lambs."
> —JOHN 21:15, EMPHASIS ADDED

Notice the question Jesus asks right off the bat: "Do you love me *more than these*?" Our love for Him is to be established higher than our love for others and ourselves. Having our love life in order—God, our spouse, ourself—enables us to follow His example of love. The example of God's love is sacrificial commitment.

> This is my command: Love each other as I have loved you. The greatest love a person can show is to die for his friends.
> —JOHN 15:13

Being a person of commitment ushers us through the difficulties of life. We are ready not just to die, but more importantly, we die for someone else. Marriage means we must be willing to submit and commit.

Paul wrote to the church of Ephesus concerning marriage. (See Ephesians 5:22–32.) In his letter he admonished the husband to love and the wife to submit like Christ and His church. By the same token, Paul was looking to anchor the attention of his readers directly on Jesus.

In essence, when Paul wrote, "Husbands, love your wife, even as

Christ also loved the church, and gave himself for it" (Eph. 5:25), he was asking, "What do you think of Christ?" In other words, if we have a *reverence* for Christ, He becomes our *reference* in life. Once we lose our reverence, we lose our reference. When we reverence God we develop a deep and profound devotion to Him. Loving God causes us to commit to our spouse and display the quality of devotion they deserve.

God commands us to come to Him with our whole hearts. When we come to Him, He then commissions us to reach out to others (starting at home) with His undying love. Consider marriage a mountain. Only through commitment will we reach the summit.

As for me, I never could bring myself to throw my fish back in the water, much to the dismay of my fishing companion. And even more, I won't throw away the love I possess in my heart for my Lord and my wife.

When I finally caught my wife and reeled her in, it was not for sport, it was for keeps. Amazingly, my wife shares the same conviction. I was elated to be her catch and a keeper. *Only God knows why she kept this old barracuda.*

Decide to be faithful. Declare the right words concerning your marriage. Remember your devotion to God creates a healthy love for your spouse.

Be committed! Since you have to play—play for keeps.

CONTENTMENT

Satisfaction is not going after something,
but rather Someone.

When Is Enough, Enough?

CONTENTMENT

Chapter Two

One Saturday morning after getting my hair cut, my barber and friend walked me to my car. We were finishing a conversation that had begun in the barber's chair. Just as I was pulling out of my parking spot, my barber indicated the tires on my car looked low.

I hopped out of the car to take a look. His automobile prowess exceeded mine. I had not noticed anything unusual with my tires. I thanked him, nonetheless, and took off without any care.

During my next visit to the barbershop, my barber inspected my tires. He asked with a half grin posted on his face, "Did you ever take care of your tires?" "No!" was the response I yielded while pulling away in my vehicle.

The following week, much to my chagrin, I found myself *on the side of the road* at night fixing a flat. This ordeal could have easily been avoided if I had heeded the warnings given weeks in advance.

Marriage is much like the vehicles we drive. It needs the proper maintenance in order to operate smoothly. Since this is so, my question for you is: "Have you checked the tires of your marriage lately?" If you are wondering how to detect low marriage tires, allow me to enlighten you.

If you are saying things like, "I'm *tired* of providing for my family"; "I'm *tired* of cleaning my house"; "I'm *tired* of caring for the children"; "I'm *tired* of my spouse"; or "I'm *tired*—I'm *tired*—I'm *tired*," such statements are indicators of low marital tires and possibly a flat marriage.

In order to avoid a marital flat each spouse *must be satisfied*.

THE DANGER OF DISSATISFACTION

No matter how you slice it, couples who are satisfied in life enjoy fulfillment in their marriage. Therefore, the goal would seem apparent. If we are to enjoy lifelong unions with our spouses, we must become content in every area of our lives.

Mark it down; when couples live in perpetual dissatisfaction, their marriage soon becomes stagnate, stifled, and stale. When a marriage undergoes stagnation, the couple no longer seems to have time for each other. Subsequently, their communication is stifled.

To stifle a couple's communication is to cut off the mainline of their intimacy. Dissatisfaction causes a loss of focus on the most important matter—connecting with your spouse. When something is stifled, it is silenced. Marital partners should not remain permanently silent. A lack of communication can cause a marriage to become stale.

Stale marriages are hard and brittle. At this point hearts are hardened and anything can cause conflict. For that reason, it is important for married couples to maintain their sense of satisfaction.

> But every man is tempted, when he is drawn away of *his own lust*, and enticed. Then when lust hath conceived, it bringeth forth sin: and sin, when it is finished, bringeth forth death.
>
> —JAMES 1:14–15, KJV, EMPHASIS ADDED

Too many marriages are murdered and sent to matrimonial morgues because of the enemy called *lust*. We live in a society that conveys the desire for more and more. The question becomes "When is enough, enough?" We are bombarded with advertisements: "Drive this!" "Live here!" "Wear this!" All these campaigns promise us satisfaction. Remember, satisfaction is not going after something but rather Someone (Jesus).

The Bible depicts the children of God as sheep. However, this world (and all its trappings) is out to make us pigs.

Luke 15:11–32 records the life of a young man who went to his father. Due to his lust, he demanded his father surrender his inheritance.

After filling his insatiable appetite, the young man found himself reduced to penury. Even worse, he ate with pigs.

There is a fact concerning pigs that needs to be mentioned. It is physically impossible for pigs to look up to the sky. In like manner, behaving like pigs prohibits us from looking up and giving God thanks. Instead, our heads are stuck and our necks become stiff. We plow ahead looking to devour everything and anyone in our paths. No marriage can survive when pigs are in it. The danger of dissatisfaction is eventually you and your spouse become disconnected.

> I have learned to be satisfied with the things I have and with everything that happens. I know how to live when I am poor, and I know how to live when I have plenty. I have learned the secret of being happy at any time in everything that happens, when I have enough to eat and when I go hungry, when I have more than I need and when I do not have enough. I can do all things through Christ, because he gives me strength.
>
> —PHILIPPIANS 4:11–13

Marriages that should flourish are sometimes filled with frustration and failure. However, when couples truly comprehend the power of contentment their marriage will not succumb to the seductive works of Satan.

DISSATISFACTION GETS YOU NOWHERE

Being dissatisfied can cause us great harm. In the pursuit of positions and possessions, we can lose those who matter most in our lives. The love in every marriage is preserved through contentment.

There was a couple in the Bible who shared the kind of love dreams are made of; at least on the surface it looked that way. Jacob and Rachel's courtship resembled a picture-book love story. However, in the midst of star gazing, taking romantic walks, and Jacob laboring for the girl of his dreams, Rachel wrestled with discontentment.

Rachel had it all. She was stunning! The Bible describes her as lovely in form and beautiful in the face. (See Genesis 29:17, NIV.) I can imagine when Rachel walked home from school the boys fought to carry her books. On the other hand, plain looking Leah (Rachel's older sister) had to carry the boy's books in order to keep company.

Due to her beauty, Rachel was accustomed to getting her way. Her encounter with Jacob would prove to be no exception. When Jacob saw her it was love at first sight. When he kissed her for the first time, he cried (Gen. 29:11).

Verses 16–29 tell us more of the story. Wasting no time, Jacob went to Rachel's father asking for her hand in marriage. In those days, it was customary for the man to offer gifts to his future bride's father. Jacob had no dowry so he agreed to work seven years without pay in order to have Rachel as his bride.

After working seven long years and getting to know Rachel better, the moment of truth had arrived for Jacob. He was wedded under a dark tent; his wife was covered from head to feet. Her face was shielded with wedding garb. That night was spent with fiery passion as the newlyweds consummated their union.

At daybreak chicanery was revealed. Jacob's father-in-law had tricked him into marrying Leah, the oldest daughter, instead of Rachel, the promised one. Remember, when Jacob kissed Rachel for the first time he cried (in joy); in this case, when he saw Leah he cried (in disappointment).

This was not only Jacob's honeymoon, it was also Leah's. Just think of how heartbroken she must have felt by her husband's rejection. Even though rejected, Leah never complained. Jacob went back to his father-in-law and struck a new deal to work seven more years without pay for the woman he desired. He loved Rachel so much the Scriptures record those fourteen years were as a few days to him (v. 20).

One would think Rachel would be a satisfied woman after all the affection, fuss, and attention that was given her, but she wasn't. My friend, dissatisfaction gets us nowhere! If not careful, we can thwart our spouse's good intentions because we lust for what others have. Jacob loved Rachel more than anything or anyone. However, his first wife, Leah, gave him children and Rachel (the love of his life) could not, and Rachel was jealous.

Tired of her condition, Rachel complained to Jacob demanding,

"Give me children, or I will die" (30:1). Rachel held Jacob in contempt because she was unsatisfied. Now, here's a man who worked fourteen years to receive this woman only to hear her say, "I want out of this marriage," or "I would rather be dead if I can't get my way."

Jacob and Rachel's dream marriage became a nightmare. Nights once filled with pleasure turned to painstaking arguments. One evening Jacob lost his cool and shouted, "Can I do what only God can do? He is the one who has kept you from having children!" (v. 2).

In time Rachel directed her dissatisfaction toward Leah. Rachel made her servant compete with Leah to see who could birth more children. Leah, who never once complained to her husband, was now in the center of marriage madness. In fact, the first time the word *praise* is mentioned in the Bible is through this horrid account. Leah, never receiving the attention from her husband despite giving him sons, named her fourth son Judah and said, "I will Praise the LORD!" (29:35).

We could all learn a lesson from Leah. When times are tough and the circumstances are not going in our favor, don't complain; just praise the Lord.

Rachel's bitter jealousy was on display again when she propositioned Leah for her mandrakes. Mandrakes were considered the aphrodisiac of that day. As a matter of fact, the nickname for them was "love apples." Rachel could have gotten her own mandrakes, but she wanted what belonged to her sister. Leah capitulated to Rachel in exchange for Jacob's company that evening. Now Rachel stooped to barter her husband's affections just to meet her own desires (30:14–15).

We could really go on with how the lack of satisfaction drove Rachel from one petty pursuit to another. However, my goal is not to mock Rachel nor drag her name through the mud. My aim is to merely highlight through this matriarch the danger of living an unsatisfied life.

God finally gave Rachel what she wanted. She had a son of her own. She named this long awaited gift Joseph. Joseph's name means *God will add*. In essence, Rachel was saying, "God give me more!" (See Genesis 30:24.) At this point I'm compelled to ask, "When is enough, enough?" This woman kicked and cried to have a son and the minute God granted her request, she asked for more.

Eventually Jacob had more wealth than his father-in-law. He had so much stuff he was forced to leave his father-in-law's house. While leaving the house, Rachel stole the family idols (31:19). Tradition mandated that the owner of these artifacts inherited the bulk of the father's possessions. As if her husband's wealth was not enough, Rachel wanted more.

Finally, God gave her a second son, surely she would be happy. Notwithstanding, Rachel named this child Benoni meaning *child of my sorrows* and she died (35:18). Look at that! A woman with a silver platter life said she was full of sorrows.

Let's examine Jacob's instructions to his family to gain insight on the results of living a life of discontentment.

> And he charged them, and said unto them, I am to be gathered unto my people: bury me with my fathers in the cave that is in the field of Ephron the Hittite.
>
> There *they buried* Abraham and Sarah his wife; there *they buried* Isaac and Rebekah his wife; and there *I buried* Leah.
>
> —Genesis 49:29, 31, kjv, emphasis added

Just in case you missed it, let me tell you. In this family plot we find Jacob's grandparents, his parents, and even his wife Leah who Jacob personally placed there. Amazingly, who is missing? Rachel. So, where is Rachel? Rachel was buried alone *on the side of the road* (35:19). Apparently, dissatisfaction gets us nowhere.

In her marriage she constantly complained and grew increasingly tired of everyone and everything. A lack of satisfaction for life caused her to become tired. In the end she was on the side of the road.

In life Jacob chose sassy. In death he chose satisfied. In essence, Jacob left Rachel, the pretty one, on the side of the road and decided that he would rest in peace with Leah.

That night as I sat on the side of the road changing the tire on my car, I learned an invaluable lesson. The next time I'm given warning about my tires or my marriage, I won't procrastinate. As a matter of fact, I make a point of consistently checking the tire pressure of my car and my marriage. My friend, I admonish you to do the same.

COOPERATION

None of us can do what all of us can do.

We're Better Together

COOPERATION

Chapter Three

One old stubborn mule said to the other old stubborn mule, "Hey, you dope; can't you see we are tied to the same piece of rope?" The other mule replied, "Yes, I see, but today you're going to come with me and we are going to eat hay over here, you see." The first mule responded, "No, you're going with me; and today we are going to eat hay over there, you see!"

So they fused and they fought and they kicked up the dirt. And, my oh my, how the rope did hurt. Then said the first mule, "Why are we acting just like those old stubborn human fools? Let's work together!" The other mule responded, "What do you mean?" The first mule reasoned, "I mean you come with me, then I'll go with thee; and together we can eat hay over here and there, you see!"

So, they ate their hay and they liked it too. They said, "We are brothers through and through." As the sun went down, they were heard to say, "Why this has been a marvelous, wonderful, beautiful day. When we two old stubborn mules decided, we can work together."

There is nothing more rewarding than when couples discover they are better together. Too many people are in marriages with a single person's attitude. In other words, there's a *what's-in-it-for-me* mentality destroying a *what's-better-for-us* reality. Sadly, too many marriages falter because couples fail to realize a fundamental concept. This concept holds the key to a successful marriage.

We must count "Me" out is the most vital concept in marriage. In fact, statements like, "What's in it for me?" or "What have you done for me lately?" just won't do. Remember, for marriage to succeed "Me" must be replaced with "We." In marriage our hearts should convey *what's best for the rest*. Take a moment and look at the word *marriage* and discover what the outside letters spell: MARRIAGE.

Did you see it? The two letters on the outside of marriage is ME.

Now let's do one more exercise. Place the letters ME in the middle of marriage to see what it spells: ARR**ME**IAG.

I think you'll agree when ME is placed in the middle of marriage we end up with a mess. In fact, the first two letters in **MESS** is ME. As long as we keep ME where it belongs, our marriage will look the way God desires it to look.

In order to possess what God intended for your marriage, you and your spouse will have to operate from the spirit of cooperation.

A PARTNER GIVES HELP

> It's better to have a partner than go it alone. Share the work, share the wealth. And if one falls down, the other helps, But if there's no one to help, tough!
> —ECCLESIASTES 4:9–10, THE MESSAGE

When we consider couples who helped each other Aquila and Priscilla are the ideal examples. Some of their story is told in Acts 18. First of all, this couple faced their share of challenges. Aquila was born into the Jewish culture. Some theologians believe Priscilla to have been a Gentile because her name is a Gentile name. They both became devout Christians, which would mean for Aquila certainly, turning his back on his Jewish rites and religion. An interracial union with diverse upbringings might implicate disaster from the start. However, this was not the case.

This couple had to endure restarting their business again and again because of continual prejudiced threats against Jews. They had to move from Rome to Corinth and then eventually back to Rome. Regrettably, many marriages have crumbled under far less pressure.

What caused this couple to persevere? How were they able to constantly stick out their necks without going for one another's throats? They operated through an egalitarian union. This is important because equality keeps a relationship healthy and growing. Through shared responsibility they helped one another through their trials.

Aquila and Priscilla's helpful attitude in business and marriage progressed to their ministry. This congenial couple was so helpful that Paul encouraged them to join him on occasions as he conducted his missionary work (Acts 18:18). This couple was inseparable. When you thought of one, you couldn't help but think of the other. They studied and grew in the Word of God together as they privately instructed mighty men in the faith such as Apollos. Apollos was a strong orator and filled with the power of God. However, it was Aquila and Priscilla who instructed him in the ways of God in a more perfect manner. (See Acts 18:24–26.)

If we can learn to work together in our marriages, like Aquila and Priscilla, God can bless our union and use it to bless many. It's wonderful when couples can cooperate. Cooperation begins with the understanding none of us can do what all of us can do.

Marriage holds the final stage of a three-phase progression.

1. We begin as *dependent* beings. As dependents we understand we need others to survive.

2. We develop into *independent* individuals. As independents we are able to handle many situations on our own.

3. We operate through *interdependence*. Within interdependence we come to appreciate how we need each other to survive.

If you haven't been helpful toward your spouse, it's not too late. Begin working on your cooperation skills. Start by doing projects around the house with your spouse. Andrea and I created what we call a job jar. We place in a jar a list of chores that need our attention. Every month we pull from the jar and tackle that specific task. The key is we must do it together. Also, you can place treats in the jar, like going to your favorite restaurant or catching a movie. This way the jar is not deemed "The dreaded jar." Just remember, the point is to do it together.

> They called to their partners in the other boat to come and help them.
>
> —LUKE 5:7

Another way of expressing the concept of help is through synergy. *Synergy* is defined as two or more agents working together to produce a result not obtainable by any of the agents independently.

Energy can be defined as the ability to exert one's self whether pushing or pulling against the forces of nature. Marriage was never designed for the act of energy to be dominating. Marriage was intended for two people to combine their energy through synergy. When God created mankind, He commanded them to be fruitful and multiply. In essence, God had synergy in mind.

Here's an interesting note: the devil is not introduced into Scripture until Eve steps on the scene. As long as Adam was by himself, only energy was available. Albeit, when Eve was created there was the possibility of synergy; thus the power to reproduce became available. Recall that synergy is at least two agents (in this case people) producing results that one cannot do alone. Don't forget, God created Eve to be a help for Adam.

Couples are better together! This is why God said, "It is not good that the man should be alone" (Gen. 2:18, KJV). The devil came to separate or isolate because he understands the power that two can create.

A turkey was speaking with a bull: "I would love to get to the top of that tree," sighed the turkey, "but I haven't got the energy." "Well," replied the bull, "why don't you nibble on some of my droppings? They're packed with nutrients."

The turkey pecked at a lump of dung and discovered it gave him enough strength to reach the lowest branch of the tree. The next day, after eating more dung, he reached the middle branch. Finally, after several nights he was proudly perched at the top of the tree. Suddenly, he was spotted by a hunter who shot him out of the tree. The moral of the story: BS might get you to the top, but it won't keep you there.

God has given us a spouse in life to serve as a partner; and through helping one another, we can make it to the top and remain there.

A Partner Gives Healing

Two in a bed warm each other. Alone, you shiver all night.
—Ecclesiastes 4:11, The Message

Within marriage there's a partner for healing and this is a comforting concept. No one wants pain. We all try to avoid suffering. Ironically, it is through pain and suffering we are made whole. Think about it, grapes must be crushed to make wine. Wheat must be crushed to make bread. Sometimes our hopes and dreams can get crushed. However, life's growing pains can make us whole. God has given us people in our lives to aid in these times of misfortune.

Consider Gomer, whose story is told in Hosea 1–3. She was beloved by her husband Hosea. Their marriage began with stimulating interest in one another. However, Hosea's future pointed toward preaching and Gomer's past was polluted with prostitution. Hosea was focused on connecting to his future while Gomer focused on connecting to her past. Therefore, their marriage progressed like a butterfly with hiccups (up and down, in and out).

Although married to Hosea, Gomer had two children outside of their union. Her daughter's name was Loruhamah, which means *unloved*, implying she would never know the love of her natural father. Her son's name was Lo-ammi, which means *no kin of mine*. The names of her children revealed Gomer's adulterous behavior to all.

Finally, Gomer left her husband to run off with a man. Chasing passion, all she found was pain. In the end, the man left Gomer desperate, destitute, and in despair. Gomer's dreadful decisions took her from sex to slavery. Gomer was crushed, but she had someone who cared.

Hosea had every right to cut her loose, but he didn't. Instead of seeking to hurt, he endeavored to heal. Hosea paid to free his wife from slavery. He brought her home and reaffirmed his love. His heart was not to replace her, it was to repair her.

> I did it. I paid good money to get her back. It cost me the price of a slave. Then I told her, "From now on you're living with me. No more whoring, no more sleeping around. You're living with me and I'm living with you."
> —Hosea 3:2–3, The Message

There are times couples don't agree with one another. These times may cause disputes and disrespect. In these cases, each needs to have a heart to heal and not cause further hurt. The quickest way to provide healing for your spouse is through forgiveness.

When we love and forgive, we are most like God. When your spouse does something to offend you, it is paramount to forgive. Don't struggle with such notions as fairness and whether they are deserving of forgiveness. We all have been forgiven by God and none of us deserve it. God's grace allows us to make mistakes without condemnation. Therefore, we should extend the same grace to our spouse.

When you truly are operating in partnership, you look to heal. A hurting partner doesn't create a healthy marriage.

I can recall when I went through combat training in the army. An essential element of that training was learning how to apply first aid to my comrades in arms. I remember spending hours discovering how to apply a tourniquet to an open wound. The tourniquet ensured my partner wouldn't lose excessive blood and eventually die. Forgiveness is the tourniquet for your marriage. You can't wait! Apply it whenever needed so your union won't die.

The central concept about combat training is looking out for the well-being of a fellow soldier. The military instructors assigned soldiers to work in pairs. Each soldier was given a Battle Buddy. Well, it's no different in marriage. We are given Battle Buddies in marriage to ensure healing when we're hurting. This is the power of two!

When God decided to destroy the earth, He had a reconstruction plan. God commanded Noah to load the ark with every beast and fowl. He took them into the ark two by two (Gen. 7:9, 15). If God healed the earth through the power of two, He will heal your marriage similarly.

A grateful convert walked over sixty miles to bring a simple gift to the missionary who had led him to Christ. The gift was not expensive, because the poor convert had little of the world's goods to give. When the missionary saw the simple gift, she received it with joy, but she offered her convert a small rebuke: "You should not have walked so far to bring me this gift." "Ah," said the convert, "the walk is part of the gift."

A partner who heals doesn't mind making sacrifices. If we are not careful, we can overlook the simple service our spouse may offer by seeking for the grander favors.

Partners are there to heal. When healing takes place the marriage is made stronger.

A PARTNER GIVES HEART

> By yourself you're unprotected. With a friend you can face the worst.
> —ECCLESIASTES 4:12, THE MESSAGE

The devil attempts to bring division in marriages through making each spouse feel alone. He too heard God announce, "It is not good for the man to be alone" (Gen. 2:18). Therefore, his plan has been to cause division within the marital union. We see this with Adam and Eve (Gen. 3:12–13), Job and his wife (Job 2:9–10), Ananias and Sapphira (Acts 5:1–3), and, unfortunately, many other couples. Have you ever heard the saying, "Together we stand; divided we fall"? Having a partner gives you the heart to stand and face life's challenges.

When you hear that voice saying your spouse is insignificant, that's the voice of the devil. Far too long there have been discussions concerning superiority in marriage. To ask the question "Who is more important in marriage, the husband or the wife?" is asinine. This would be like asking a pilot, "Which wing is more important on a plane, the right or the left?" It's obvious both wings are equally important if flight is going to be successful. So it is with marriage, both partners are significant.

It has to be understood that if your marriage is to be successful, thriving, and increasing in the will of God, it takes two! Am I suggesting that a person cannot succeed in life on their own? Certainly not! However, when you are married you must develop cooperation.

> How should one chase a thousand, and two put ten thousand to flight?
> —DEUTERONOMY 32:30, KJV

Think with me, the very notion of the previous scripture is not only multiplication, it is miraculous! Again, the scripture reads that one could chase a thousand. What's more, two can make ten thousand flee. The point is there is strength in numbers.

Many marriages are neutered and rendered ineffective because the couple tries to accomplish goals independent of each other. Let's take the mathematical operation of multiplication. First of all, to have multiplication takes multiples (this begins with the power of two). When you multiply the number zero to any other number the result is zero. When you multiply the number one to any other number the result is always the other number. Now, the actual increase in multiplication begins at the number two. There is power in two! Your increase comes as your partner gives you heart. This is to say they encourage you to give you courage.

I recall times when I felt inadequate. However, Andrea was there giving me that shot of confidence I needed to push me through. I have returned the favor whenever she needed it.

Years ago she and I set out to purchase our first home. Neither of us knew the process of buying a home nor were we aware of the painstaking letdown that lay ahead. I remember hearing from God as He told us to step out by faith. And believe me it had to be faith because we both lacked the financial means to buy a house.

When the time came to close on the house, something went wrong and the deal fell through. Overwhelmed with feelings of failure, I told Andrea we had to renege on the entire endeavor. Suddenly, with boldness that I had never witnessed in Andrea, she spoke with authority. She said we were not going to back down but press our way forward. Needless to say, God made a move that caused our heads to spin. We got the house! More importantly, I learned that partners give heart.

When couples collaborate with their resources, hearts, and minds, God gets involved. Look at the account of Jonathan and his armor bearer. Although they were not a married couple, the principle still applies. These two men faced off with a Philistine garrison and experienced tremendous success. Consider the following passage:

> And Jonathan said to the young man that bare his armour,
> Come, and let us go over unto the garrison of these
> uncircumcised: it may be that the LORD will work for us:
> for there is no restraint to the LORD to save by many or by

few. And his armourbearer said unto him, Do all that is in thine heart: turn thee; behold, I am with thee according to thy heart.

—1 Samuel 14:6–7, kjv

Only two men defeated an entire army because, as Jonathan put it, the Lord worked for them. In fact, what culminated the event and provoked God's involvement was not what Jonathan said but rather what his armor bearer proclaimed. Did you miss it? Well, let's look at it again:

Behold, I am with thee *according* to thy heart.

—1 Samuel 14:7, kjv, emphasis added

Did you see it this time? The word *according* was the activator that moved the hand of God on their behalf. The term *accord* is a musical term meaning harmony and agreement. In essence, when we have cooperation fully expressed in our marriage, we have the heavenly host standing behind, beside and before us.

Two people will not walk together unless they have *agreed* to do so.

—Amos 3:3, emphasis added

Also, I tell you that if two of you on earth *agree* about something and pray for it, it will be done for you by my Father in heaven.

—Matthew 18:19, emphasis added

Too often couples operate in arrangement but not agreement. *Arrangement* means to place things in order. *Agreement* means to place order in things. Jonathan's armor bearer gave him heart to face the Philistines and Andrea gave me heart to face our situation.

You should know your spouse and you are better together. If you don't know this, or somewhere between saying your wedding vows and where you are now you have forgotten this, start meditating on the fact that a partner gives help, healing, and heart. Allow this to become your mantra: "We are better together!" As you repeat this and act upon your confession, you will discover what the mules in the opening anecdote of this chapter discovered. We, as married couples, can work together!

CHEERFULNESS

Don't seek to have a spouse in your life;
seek to have life in your spouse

CHEERFULNESS

Chapter Four

The king of a particular country traveled often; but one day a man living near the palace remarked to a friend, "Well, it looks like the king is home tonight." "How do you know?" asked the friend. The man pointed up toward the royal house. "Because when the king is home," he said, "the castle is all lit up."

A pivotal key to a healthy marriage is not to seek a spouse in your life, but rather desire life in your spouse. Marriages with Jesus in the center are lit with the love of God, and that light exudes joy. Jesus causes us to have joy in our attitude. I have heard it said that happiness is an emotion and joy is an attitude. Emotions come and go, but attitudes come and grow. It's been stated, "A man's home is his castle." However, will his castle and his marriage be lit with the joy of his presence?

Here's a fact, some people brighten a room just by walking out of it. I don't know about you, but I desire to brighten a room when I walk into it. In order to brighten a place as well as people we must be cheerful. Cheerful people cheer up people!

Cheerfulness is a medicine that will add life to your marriage. There is a lot of talk about the fictitious fountain of youth. Well, I know not of any fountains that cause you to remain young. However, the right attitude causes vitality, and that attitude is joy. Your marriage will have life and vitality through cheerfulness.

BE THE CHEERLEADER

When you possess the right attitude about your marriage, you receive the right results in your marriage. Joy allows you to place your spouse above yourself. Joy enables you to think and act according to a three-step process. First, you think of Jesus. Second, you think of others (in marriage, your spouse). Third, you think of yourself.

Jesus is the reason you have joy

Others become the recipients of your joy

You are responsible to maintain your joy

Couples who maintain joy in their home create an environment that is conducive for love to grow. Knowing this, it is imperative that you maintain a high level of joy. Therefore, become the cheerleader in your marriage. This means you don't wait for your spouse to make you happy, you determine in your heart you will have joy.

The cheerleader understands each day belongs to the Lord. Also, God's plan for us is not finished. Therefore, if you do not like your present condition, do not fret or frown. Know that better days are ahead. A marriage with all sunshine becomes a desert. A marriage with all rain becomes a swamp. In light of this, both sunny and rainy days make a well-balanced marriage.

A cheerleader is willing and able to lead with cheer. The cheerleader does not seek accolades or attention. Their desire is to keep the team's spirit up. Whenever I'm watching a sports event like football, it interests me to see the cheerleaders come out on the field. The cheerleaders are interesting because no matter what the score is, their enthusiasm remains positive and fired up. When the home team appears to be losing, the cheerleader never waits for the outcome to start cheering. We should do the same in our marriage. No matter what happens, our desire should be to keep up the marriage morale and press on until we get the outcome we desire.

Wake up every morning declaring, "This is the day that the Lord has made; I will rejoice and be glad in it" (Ps. 118:24). I often ask my wife before 9 a.m., "How is your day?" At first she would look at me puzzled. Then she would add, "My day hasn't started yet." I would follow up with this: determine now your day is good no matter what challenges it may present. I love to give my wife the option of optimism.

I figured out long ago that I can be a cheerleader or a party pooper.

I decided the life of a cheerleader. The cheerleader's job brings great benefits. Therefore, that's the job for me. Many people are having *near-life-experiences.*

Those who have near-life-experiences go through life looking for encouragement, but never become the encouragers. You truly haven't lived until you have inspired someone else to accomplish their goal or catch their dream. To do this requires above all else to believe in others and to cheer them through life's trials. Everybody loves to be encouraged. When you encourage your spouse, you're helping them do better in life. Consequently, they become a better person to be around.

> Go and enjoy good food and sweet drinks. Send some to people who have none, because today is a holy day to the Lord. Don't be sad, because the joy of the LORD will make you strong.
>
> —NEHEMIAH 8:10

A woman came home, screeched her car into the driveway, ran into the house, and shouted to the top of her lungs: "Fred, pack your bags! I won the lottery!" Fred said, "That's great. What should I pack—beach stuff or mountain stuff?" The wife yelled back, "It doesn't matter, just get out!"

Some people have been in a bad marriage for so long it's hard to imagine joy and marriage in the same context. Therefore, when they find joy, they try to lose their spouse because they can't conceive having the two together. Albeit, having joy in your marriage should be perceived as a God-given pursuit.

CHEER UP! IT COULD BE WORSE

What happens when one or both spouses lack joy? Without joy, the trials that come to your marriage will affect you in a negative way. The person who does not exercise cheerfulness exposes himself to a downward spiral of oppression, depression, repression, and eventually suppression.

Let's take a moment and view each of these downward stages:

EMOTIONAL DOWNWARD SPIRAL	
Oppression	When you are placed under prolonged harsh or cruel treatment or control
Depression	A mood of hopelessness and feelings of inadequacy, experiencing a reduction in your vitality and vigor
Repression	When you are prevented from sounding off or bursting out
Suppression	To prevent from being seen or known: not acknowledged or someone wishes you do not exist

In order to ensure that you do not succumb to any of these negative downward stages, you must maintain your joy—especially when bad things happen. The way to accomplish this is to understand that bad things happen to both good and bad people. The Bible contends the rain falls on both the just and the unjust (Matt. 5:45; see also 7:24–27).

However, never forget two things:

1. God will never allow more than we can handle to come our way.

2. God will use whatever comes our way to develop us into better people.

God can take your trouble and change it into treasure. Your sorrow can be exchanged for joy, not just a momentary smile, but a deep new joy. It will be a bubbling experience of new hope that brings brightness to your eyes and a song to your heart. In the midst of darkness, you will learn lessons you might never have learned in the day. We all have seen dreams turn to ashes—ugly things, hopeless and heartbreaking—but beauty for ashes is God's exchange.

—BARBARA JOHNSON[1]

Before you start complaining about the troubles in your marriage, stop and look at it from God's perspective. If you are experiencing a season of rain in your marriage, don't be quick to leave; stick around and see the rainbow breaking through the clouds. God is looking to promote you and your spouse to a higher degree of living. Consequently, with every persecution there is promotion. Every test reveals a testimony. And in the midst of every mess comes a message:

> Give unto them beauty for ashes, the oil of joy for mourning, the garment of praise for the spirit of heaviness.
> —ISAIAH 61:3, KJV

No matter what comes your way, keep and cultivate cheerfulness in your marriage. God has given us beauty for our ashes. Therefore, when we are handed a bowl of lemons, instead of becoming cantankerous we just need to relax and make lemonade.

Beloved, understand this above all else: pain and joy are needed together. It is pain that causes us to call on the Lord. It is pain that makes us bow over to seek the face of God. It's joy that sees God's footprints in our circumstances. And joy acknowledges God's caring hands calming every storm.

Consider what God told His servant Moses concerning their unfavorable condition:

> The Lord said, "I have seen the troubles my people have suffered in Egypt, and I have heard their cries when the Egyptian masters hurt them. I am concerned about their pain, and I have come down to save them from the Egyptians."
> —EXODUS 3:7–8

So we see because of pain Israel sought the aid of God. We also see God was more than willing to help. And He delivered Israel from their oppressors. Let us read Israel's response:

> So that day the LORD saved the Israelites from the Egyptians and the Israelites saw the Egyptians lying dead

on the seashore. When the Israelites saw the great power
the Lord had used against the Egyptians, they feared the
Lord, and they trusted him and his servant Moses.

Then Moses and the Israelites sang this song to the
Lord...

—Exodus 14:30–31, 15:1

Do you have a song in your heart for God? If not, you better get one.
When God brings you through your test or trial it would do you good
to express your joy with a song. On the other hand, you don't have to
wait for God to deliver you to sing a song. It is good practice to sing a
song of joy and praise in the midst of your circumstance. This is what
Paul the apostle of the Lord did when he found himself in prison with
Silas (Acts 16:25). At midnight they began to sing and God opened the
prison doors. If this is the midnight hour in your marriage and you
need God to break some chains or open some doors, sing!

Show Your Spouse the Funny Side

All work and no play makes Jack a dull boy, and it doesn't do much
for Jill either. If you never take time out to enjoy your spouse, get
ready; your marriage is headed for a dead end. Many marriages have
imploded from the inside out due to the lack of recreation. So much
time is given to going after things when the best things in life aren't
things.

> So go eat your food and enjoy it; drink your wine and be
> happy, because that is what God wants you to do. Put on
> nice clothes and make yourself look good. Enjoy life with
> the wife you love.
>
> —Ecclesiastes 9:7–9

When you received your spouse, you received the best God has
for you. Always remember, God loves us all equally, but He doesn't
love us all the same. Practically speaking, God knows what it takes to
please you and He's placed those qualities in your spouse.

You may ask, "Why haven't I seen these qualities in my spouse?"

More than likely, you have seen them, just not lately. If you fall in that category, do not get discouraged. Your marriage might be like a scattered jigsaw puzzle; the picture is there. However, right now it's in pieces and needs to be put back together. A surefire way to get your marriage moving in the right direction is through times of refreshing.

Couples need to take advantage of leisure time as often as possible. Leisure time allows couples to reflect on their values. The truth is this; the grind of life can suck the sap right out of our marriages.

Andrea and I have been fortunate to see the world together. No matter where we are, we take time to pause and reflect on the goodness of God. Then we consider how we relate to one another. This time of reflection is difficult when you're working. Therefore, it does the marriage good to take time out to play. Now, for some the term *play* sounds too childish. So let me say it this way: play—play—play! Maturity is good, but don't become so old that your marriage dies. You should purpose in your heart that for your marriage there will be *no more bored meetings*. Whether traveling abroad or staying home, you and your spouse need to meet each other with enthusiasm about spending life together.

When was the last time your spouse saw your smile or heard you laugh? Can you recall the last time you witnessed a smile on your spouse's face? Or even still, when was the last time you caused a smile on your spouse's face? If I look up sad sack or sourpuss, will I see a photo of you?

> A happy heart is like good medicine, but a broken spirit drains your strength.
>
> —PROVERBS 17:22

Have you ever laughed until your face began hurting? If so, that's an indicator that you don't laugh enough. In case you didn't know, fifteen facial muscles are used when we laugh. And these muscles need a daily workout. Many marriages are sick due to the lack of this medicine called laughter.

Now, more than ever before, you need to show your spouse your funny side. This is one of your better qualities and should not be left dormant. Go get a good joke book and practice making your spouse laugh. I'm willing to bet this will add years to your marriage. More important, it will add *good* years to your marriage.

In the Bible, Isaac and Rebekah were a cheerful couple. The name Isaac means "God laughs." The Scripture reveals that Isaac loved Rebekah deeply, and her love for him comforted him when his mother died (Gen. 24:67). This couple's fondness and their playful attitudes toward each other were witnessed by a king who, the Bible records, saw Isaac "sporting" with his wife (Gen. 26:8, KJV).

My friend, keep your marriage healthy by expressing cheerfulness. Remember; make the first move by becoming the cheerleader in your relationship. Remind yourself and your spouse to cheer up no matter what the circumstances. And you do have a funny side so show it more—play more!

My wife and I are a dynamic duo. Even more, we are a congenial couple. We decided the lights will remain on in our castle. Our light is joy. Therefore, we will have no more bored meetings. How about you?

PURITY

The closer we are to God the purer our life becomes.

Glow in the Dark

PURITY

Chapter Five

An old missionary sought to teach his new convert how to genuinely have a hunger for Jesus. As the convert desired this priceless lesson, the venerable missionary led him to a nearby lake. Once they were both positioned in the lake, the missionary took hold of the convert and held him head first under the water. Soon the convert began running out of breath so he attempted to resurface. However, the missionary relentlessly kept him under. After minutes had passed, the missionary allowed the convert to reemerge. As the convert was panting for air, the missionary admonished him, "When you want God as much as you wanted air, you shall have Him along with a purified life."

Marriage may not be heaven, but it can be a haven for couples. The world's negative influence will attach to us if we are not cognizant of its power and presence. This adverse influence can eventually turn a decent marriage into one filled with decadence. As a result, we will find ourselves as the convert in the opening vignette gasping for air.

God has made us to be lights in a world full of darkness. Therefore, it's imperative that we shine our lights. Purity is the brightest light that we can shine. Purity is the ability to remain clean. Purity seeks the truth. To put it plainly, purity is getting closer to God. Marriages are made better when God is in the center. I'm not speaking about mere church attendance. I'm talking about having an authentic presence of God in the marriage. His presence is genuinely felt when we allow His Word to influence our attitudes.

A lot of people suffer through marriages. Infidelity, bickering, covetousness, malice, and anger are some impurities which cause pain. It's these acts of uncleanness that ruin otherwise good marriages. Impurities drive us away from God and consequently farther away from our spouse. Thus, to have the quality of marriage the Lord intended, we must stay close to Him.

The closer we are to God the purer our life becomes. Remember, God will not allow us to stay around Him long without our lives being purified. God's glory burns up anything that is not pure. God told Moses that His presence would consume Israel because of their lack of purity.

> But I won't be with you in person—you're such a stubborn, hard-headed people!—lest I destroy you on the journey... GOD said to Moses, "Tell the Israelites, 'You're one hard-headed people. I couldn't stand being with you for even a moment—I'd destroy you. So take off all your jewelry until I figure out what to do with you.'" So the Israelites stripped themselves of their jewelry from Mount Horeb on.
>
> —EXODUS 33:3, 5–6, THE MESSAGE

God's presence is consuming. When Moses asked to see God's glory, he had to be covered by God's hand (Exod. 33:20–23). After his encounter with God, Moses' face glowed.

> When Moses came down from Mount Sinai carrying the two Tablets of The Testimony, he didn't know that *the skin of his face glowed because he had been speaking with* GOD. Aaron and all the Israelites saw Moses, saw his radiant face, and held back, afraid to get close to him.
>
> —EXODUS 34:29–30, THE MESSAGE, EMPHASIS ADDED

The longer we stay in the presence of God, the more we will glow in the dark. This given glow reflects the purity in our lives. Would you like your marriage to glow? If so, stay close to God!

The term *purity* is foreign to many. It's a term we don't hear enough. We live in a society that considers truth to be a tired expression. Nowadays, couples are prone to shameless infidelity; our pro athletes are discovered having more steroids than stats; corporate banks promise investors good business while on the verge of going out of business. Somehow, all of this has become normal. Consequently, God is calling for purity. The true and only way to become pure is to have an ardent desire to come closer and closer to God.

STAND UP FOR THE SAVIOR

> All the ways of a man are clean in his own eyes; but the
> LORD weigheth the spirits.
>
> —PROVERBS 16:2, KJV

When we follow after the world's allurements, we move farther from God. It might seem innocent to buy into self-fulfilling behavior; but ask yourself, "What price am I willing to pay for these detrimental indulgences." Once Adam became impure he hid from God (Gen. 3:9). Are you willing to hide from God in order to seek pleasure? Or worse, are you willing to hide your God from others?

The following scriptures encourage us to reveal God in our actions and attitudes:

> Here's another way to put it: You're here to be light, bringing out the God-colors in the world. God is not a secret to be kept. We're going public with this, as public as a city on a hill. If I make you light-bearers, you don't think I'm going to hide you under a bucket, do you? I'm putting you on a *light stand*. Now that I've put you there on a hilltop, on a *light stand*—shine! Keep open house; be generous with your lives. By opening up to others, you'll prompt people to open up with God, this generous Father in heaven.
>
> —MATTHEW 5:14–16, THE MESSAGE, EMPHASIS ADDED

Inevitably there comes a time when we must stand up and be recognized. Purity calls for it. In fact, it is important for our spouse to know we are honest and can be trusted. If we operate dishonestly eventually it catches up to us. Your spouse must trust you wholeheartedly for your marriage to remain healthy. If they witness you double-dealing with others, eventually they suspect you of being untruthful with them.

Take Tom, who does whatever it takes to save a dollar. He has people cut his lawn only to complain they don't cut it right. No matter who is the hired work, he always grumbles that the job is wrong in order not to pay. Whenever Tom and his wife dine out, he nitpicks about the food and service, hoping for a free meal.

The Book of Proverbs warns us of such matters:

> Buyers say, "This is bad. It's no good." Then they go away and brag about what they bought…Stolen food may taste sweet at first, but later it will feel like a mouth full of gravel.
>
> —PROVERBS 20:14, 17

As of late, Tom's wife no longer enjoys his company. His dishonesty has made her uncomfortable. She asks him to stop his swindling ways. He ignores her request. He thinks it's all right to deceive people in order to save a dollar. He reasons that it's the way to get ahead in life. Tom's philosophy is "why pay when you don't have to?" Unfortunately, Tom *is* paying and he doesn't know it. In his attempts to save a dollar, dishonesty is causing him to lose his marriage. What's more, Tom is losing his relationship with the Lord.

As Christians we must have standards. The root word in *standard* is the word *stand*. When you stand up for God, your goals are clear and your path is straight. In a world filled with darkness, it is vital that we keep our light shining. Standing up for God and what is right isn't always easy. For this reason, God gives us strength to do so.

The following excerpt expresses this fact:

> Be steadfast, my boy, when you're tempted,
> To do what you know to be right.
> Stand firm by the colors of manhood,
> And you will o'ercome in the fight.
> "The right," be your battle cry ever
> In waging the warfare of life.

And God, who knows who are the heroes,
Will give you the strength for the strife.

—PHOEBE CARY[1]

STAND OUT AT SOME TIME

Have you ever driven at night and seen an oncoming car with one of its headlights out? The scene is strange and can be quite reckless. Picture the danger of a car at night without any headlights. Now, imagine a marriage in the dark with no headlights. A marriage with one or no spouse striving for purity is reckless and downright dangerous.

Being pure doesn't mean being perfect. It just means you have a heart to please God. It means you follow His commands to the best of your ability. As Christians our goal is not to be better. Nevertheless, we should be different. Can your unsaved neighbors see that your life is different from theirs?

People often ask me, "Are you related to Bishop Nate Holcomb?" I answer proudly, "Yes! He's my father." They say, "We can tell, you look just like him." Shouldn't our relationship with God be just as strong? People should ask, "Are you related to God?" If our walk with God is strong, you can bet our marriages are healthy and durable. When we reflect God's image, we stand out for Him. And through purity we can love our spouse perfectly.

One evening, a wife drew her husband's attention to the couple next door. She took him out on the porch so he could see what they were doing. Pointing across the yard, she said, "Do you see that couple? How devoted they are? He kisses her every time they are close. I notice he often brings her flowers, gifts, and dinner. Why don't you ever do that?" "I would love to," replied the husband, "but I don't know her that well."

Ask yourself, is my marriage a model for others to follow? If not, why not? Don't answer, "Times are tough." As Christians we are called to a higher standard. When times are darkest; we must shine our brightest. We must be able to glow in the dark. When we glow in the dark, we stand out.

One evening while in Hawaii, my wife and I saw the most spectacular display of stars. While enjoying a Hawaiian luau, we gazed up at the sky. Every star seemed close enough to touch. Of course, the entire scene would not be possible in the day. It was the darkness of the night that made the stars sparkle with brilliance.

When times are darkest we should rise and shine our brightest. People will see us shine through purity. More importantly, they will see the God in us. When others scheme to get ahead, the child of God will move forward by being honest. Also, stars cause us to imagine the God who created them. We should stand out sometimes and the best time is when it's dark.

A venerable older preacher took his wife to a restaurant for their anniversary. He heard how the food was delectable and the service beyond reproach. He thought their anniversary was the best time to give this well-mentioned restaurant a try.

Upon entering the place, he noticed it was unusually dark. While fumbling and stumbling they followed the maître d' to their table. Once seated, the pastor and his wife could hardly see one another's face.

After some time they were able to see each other and those who sat around their table. When their waiter appeared they thanked him for turning up the lights. The waiter's response caught the couple by surprised. He informed them the lights had never been turned up.

The reality was that the couple's eyes adjusted to the darkness. Too often when we are supposed to outshine the darkness, we merely adjust to it. Adjusting to the darkness can jeopardize the health of our marriage.

STAND FOR SOMETHING

The marriage standing on honesty has a sure foundation. Couples who are open and pure with one another and others benefit from well-lasting relationships. On the other hand, those who deceive usually suffer dire consequences.

There was a couple named Ananias and Sapphira who experienced such consequences. They lived in the days when the church experienced its birth. Their church exploded on the scene with power and pureness. The congregation of those days believed everyone was to flow with one heart and mind. Also, material possessions were shared equally without dissimulation (Acts 4:32). Decisions were made for the mutual care and concern of the congregation as a whole. The result of this cohesiveness was God's blessings on their church.

This movement of God attracted this divisive couple. Ananias and Sapphira saw opportunity for chicanery and they took it. Their dishonesty was not warranted due to lack or need. Sapphira's name means "beautiful" or "sapphire." She was named after the precious stone that bestows such beauty. The name Ananias means "Yahweh has dealt graciously." They had good looks and God's good hand on their life. Needless to say, they had a lot going for them.

What would make this couple risk and eventually ruin their integrity? In a congregation like theirs they were already accepted. However, being accepted wasn't enough, they wanted to receive adulation. They wanted more than membership; their eyes were set on being spiritual monuments. In essence, they craved the praise of men. This is what threatens purity the most. When we desire the accolades of men, purity usually takes the backseat in our lives. Approval is good, but not at the expense of purity.

John Wooden remarked:

> Be more concerned with your character than with your reputation, because your character is what you really are, while your reputation is merely what others think you are.[2]

Ananias and Sapphira witnessed people being appreciated through acts of generosity. They wanted the same response without committing the same sacrifices. Many were giving their possessions and trusting the Lord to meet their needs. Ananias and Sapphira could not or would not trust God that way. Therefore, they conspired with one another to deceive the church.

They too sold private property. However, they hid some of the proceeds from their sale and lied by saying they gave all to the church (Acts 5:1–2). Their sin was not holding back any money; it was theirs to keep or give away. This couple's sin was fabricating a story to impress God's people. They sold their property for one price and changed the price on their receipt to a smaller number. They took the receipt to

God's minister Peter and pretended to give the full sale amount. God revealed to Peter the couple's chicanery.

> Peter said, "Ananias, how did Satan get you to lie to the Holy Spirit and secretly keep back part of the price of the field? Before you sold it, it was all yours, and after you sold it, the money was yours to do with as you wished. So what got into you to pull a trick like this? You didn't lie to men but to God."
>
> —Acts 5:3–4, The Message

Can you imagine this couple's relationship? Attempting to deceive God must take a lot of nerve. I dare to say, this was not a first offense or one-time affair. They had done this kind of thing before but maybe not on this level. Albeit, you might get away with dishonesty for a while, but sooner or later it catches up to you.

Their marriage was cut short as they both dropped dead in the church for their equal part in this duplicitous deed (Acts 5:5–6, 10). We can look at the life of this couple and learn. Or we can ignore their mistake and eventually share their fate.

Which is more valuable—having the appearance of a spiritual walk with God or to really become like God? Through purity we can walk with God and leave hypocrisy behind.

The Bible gives record of a man named Enoch. He walked with God and one day he was not and God took him (Gen. 5:24, kjv). We could ask, "He was not what?" Well, he was not dishonest among many other things, but he certainly was pure and this is why God took him.

The convert in our opening tale learned a valuable lesson. Air is vital for our survival. Just like air, God's presence is critical to the life of a marriage. His presence causes there to be purity in the couple.

My friend, strive to have the kind of marriage that shines through purity. Stand up for God! Stand out in a dark world! Stand for a life that is pleasing and pure to our heavenly Father. By doing this, God will add His light, life, and love to your marriage.

Through purity, we can always glow in the dark.

TEMPERANCE

Using self-restraint in our speech and our appetites.

Get a Grip

TEMPERANCE

Chapter Six

Indonesia's Mt. Tambora experienced the largest known volcanic eruption in over 1,300 years. It occurred April 10–15, 1816. The eruption of Tambora killed an estimated 92,000 people. As a direct result of the explosion and ash fall, 10,000 died. Another 82,000 died from agricultural and other related causes.

The concussion from the explosion was felt a thousand miles away. Mt. Tambora, which was more than 13,000 feet tall before the explosion, was reduced to 9,000 feet after ejecting more than ninety-three cubic miles of debris into the atmosphere.

The effects of the eruption were felt worldwide. That year of 1816 became known as The Year Without a Summer due to volcanic ash in the atmosphere that lowered worldwide temperatures. As many as 100,000 additional deaths from starvation in other areas are thought to be traced to the eruption.

As you just read, volcanic eruptions can be devastatingly horrific. Natural disasters can wipe out entire communities, and the same can be said concerning domestic ones. Domestic disasters are created through eruptions as well. However, tempers take the place of volcanoes. When people are unable to control their tempers, marriages and too often entire families are destroyed.

I find it intriguing that this massive mountain Tambora once stood 13,000 feet tall. And yet after its eruption, it was reduced to 9,000 feet. Losing our tempers can eventually diminish our status and stature. Our children can think we hung the moon and our spouse can see us as heroes. Of course, this can all dissipate if we have a pilot's license for flying off the handle.

Tambora's eruption caused 1816 to be known as The Year Without a Summer. Think about that; summer represents the season of youthfulness and vitality. Amazingly, one eruption after another can corrode our marriage and take away its summer seasons. The vigor we once enjoyed with our spouse seems more like vinegar. The summer of our marriage can turn to winter.

In the Bible there was a man named Saul. This man had it all. He had good looks and he was tall in stature (1 Sam. 9:2). Moreover, Saul was anointed to be king over God's people (10:1). He was also a great military leader, which was evidenced by his many victories in battle. However, Saul gradually lost everything he valued because he lacked control over his temper.

THERE'S TOO MUCH AT STAKE

First, we find Saul losing his temper with David. David loved and admired Saul and would have done anything for him. However, Saul's affection for David went awry because he felt David's power and popularity growing with the people.

> And from that time on Saul kept a jealous eye on David.
> —1 SAMUEL 18:9, NIV

Saul had lost control of himself on occasions, even to the point where it became deadly. David, who was faithful and loyal to Saul, lived in constant fear of his life. There were times when Saul's rage caused him to be out of character.

> David was playing the harp, as he usually did. Saul had a spear in his hand and he hurled it, saying to himself, "I'll pin David to the wall." But David eluded him twice.
> —1 SAMUEL 18:10–11, NIV

In spite Saul's barrage of threats and attempts on David's life, David maintained a degree of respect for Saul. There was a time when David had the opportunity to take Saul's life while he was sleeping and he did not. (See 1 Samuel 24:1–16.) Spouses may lose their cool with one another, but it should never come to a point where either person's life is in danger.

Saul's vitriol for David eventually spilled over on his children. First, he began throwing knives at his beloved son Jonathan (20:32–34). Then, he ruined the marriage of David to his own daughter Michal by eventually giving her away to another man (25:44).

Saul's account is a tragic one. He began his reign as Israel's first king with prominence and promise only to watch it be reduced to ashes.

Many marriages have been filled with the ash of a spouse's moody temperament and corrosive character. Relationships that could have remained healthy became sick because of bitter eruptions. Married couples cannot afford to have temper tantrums because there is too much at stake. Other lives are involved.

MANAGING MY MOOD

> Patience is better than strength. Controlling your temper
> is better than capturing a city.
>
> —PROVERBS 16:32

If there is one thing that I continue to strive for in my marriage, it is to manage my mood. A mood is a state of mind or feeling. Couples who cannot manage their moods are destined for devastation in their marriage. Things are not always going to happen the way we want them to happen. For that reason, we must be able to keep our composure.

You have to decide now, are you going to be a thermostat or a thermometer? Before you answer the previous question allow me to further explain this idea. A thermostat regulates the environment and a thermometer registers the environment. A thermostat will adjust to what is taking place, but a thermometer can only reflect what is happening.

Let's say things aren't going well at work and your boss is really coming down on you. If you are a thermostat, when you get home you make the necessary adjustments to remain calm and enjoy your family. However, if you are a thermometer, when you arrive home everyone can tell that your day went bad because of your actions.

As Christians we must learn to respond and not react to the negative things that occur in our lives. To respond means your response is a sensible one. When you react you are really manipulated through compulsion, it's called "knee-jerk." The key word in knee-jerk is *jerk*, which is often the case for those who lack self-control.

The apostle Paul says, "But I keep under my body, and bring it unto subjection" (1 Cor. 9:27, KJV). In other words, it is crucial to remain disciplined. Therefore, I manage my mood.

My wife may not do what I like all the time. I certainly don't hit the bull's-eye every time when it comes to pleasing her. Nevertheless, it does neither one of us any good to get upset and lose control. As a matter of fact, it does more harm than good. When things get heated in your marriage, that's when it's time to take the chill pill of self-control. Resist the temptation to get caught in the moment; think about your marriage. Give each other time, get a grip on yourself and the situation, and then come together and discuss fixing the problem in a rational way.

Discipline: Who Needs It?

Discipline is a synonym for self-control. Again, Paul said he had to train his body in order to get the desired results. We too have to train our bodies because as we get older it becomes more difficult to respond rather than react. The old timers call it "getting set in your ways."

We all need discipline, especially when we are married. This is true because what we do or neglect to accomplish will affect our spouse also. When we are married we must remember that our lives are not our own. We are responsible to someone else, and keep in mind that ultimately we must answer to God.

> As a prisoner for the Lord, then, I urge you to live a life worthy of the calling you have received.
> —Ephesians 4:1, NIV

Unfortunately, many people do not see marriage for what it is—a calling. Marriage is holy and thus belongs to God. Your husband and wife belong to you through relationship. However, we all belong to God through His ownership. The minute we truly comprehend and appreciate that fact our marriage will survive, it will also thrive.

David and Bathsheba were in desperate need of discipline.

Subsequently, their relationship was spawned through sin and deception. A lack of self-control placed them on a slippery slope that would prove quite deadly.

We begin this love story looking at David. He was a lion-slaying legend, a bear-killing brute, and the hero who defeated the hulk. Songs were written about the victories he brought Israel (1 Sam. 18:7). Nations trembled at the mention of his name. The Scriptures record, "All Israel and Judah loved David" (v. 16). Most of all, the Lord testifies, "I have found David...a man after my own heart" (Acts 13:22, NIV). Just when David reached the pinnacle of his life, he decided to break his discipline.

David worked hard and fought hard so he felt he deserved a break. This is when it happened! David let his guard down. The time came when kings went out to battle. David sent the captain of his army with his army, but he stayed back in Jerusalem (2 Sam. 11:1). Before we can figure maybe he stayed back for business, the Scriptures tell us that he was sleeping in days and hanging out nights (v. 2).

She was spotted! Bathsheba was a beautiful woman; but in this case, she was far from innocent. Bathsheba made no attempts to conceal her private bath time, and David saw her. He was a man that liked what he saw and was determined to get what he liked. Imagine how many marriages lay in ruin because a spouse possesses the "I-got-to-have-it" mind-set. When there is no discipline in marriage, abuse is inevitable.

Like David, when we evade our responsibility, we'll end up at the wrong place doing the wrong thing. There's an adage that goes, "An idle mind is the devil's playground." Oh, what a true statement. We must maintain the medicine of temperance in order for our marriages to remain healthy.

David sends for Bathsheba and commits adultery with her. She becomes pregnant with David's child; and what follows is a downward spiral of deceit and debauchery. Bathsheba never tells her husband, Uriah, (a faithful soldier of David's) what has taken place. David tied murder to his adultery by having Uriah killed (vv. 14–17).

If we are not disciplined, the devil will take advantage of us at every point. You may start off doing something that seems so miniscule and before it's over you're left with someone's blood on your hands. Without question, everyone needs discipline.

Consider the following caveat:

> God is strong, and he wants you strong. So take everything the Master has set out for you, well-made weapons of the best materials. And put them to use so you will be able to stand up to everything the Devil throws your way. This is no afternoon athletic contest that we'll walk away from and forget about in a couple of hours. This is for keeps, a life-or-death fight to the finish against the Devil and all his angels. Be prepared. You're up against far more than you can handle on your own. Take all the help you can get, every weapon God has issued, so that when it's all over but the shouting you'll still be on your feet.
>
> —EPHESIANS 6:10–13, THE MESSAGE

Before we can use any weapon the Lord has issued us, we must be skilled and disciplined. Above all, if we find ourselves behind enemy lines, we need to know how to get back where we belong. Again, David was a man after the heart of God. Therefore, even with all of his baggage, he knew how to humble himself and repent.

The Bible records that once his relationship with God was broken, David had no peace. Eventually he sought the Lord's forgiveness. (See 1 Samuel 12.) In the end, Bathsheba and David found favor with God, and so can we if we are willing to turn from sin and repent.

The aftermath of Mt. Tambora was death, devastation, and despair. However, after time, Indonesia and the rest of the world was able to recover from the carnage left by this monstrous eruption.

It's disheartening. Many families are left suffering because of an unchecked, tumultuous temper devouring everyone and everything in its path. There's too much at stake! Let's learn to manage our moods and through discipline experience a great marriage. If anything, allow love to erupt in your marriage and the only things that melt will be hearts.

PEACEFULNESS

Giving up the love of power to discover
the power of love.

Do Not Disturb

PEACEFULNESS

Chapter Seven

His eyes sparkled with excitement; newly wedded, he helps his beautiful bride onto the coach then he joins her on the seat. He takes the reins of the one-horse carriage and with a firm jerk they begin a pleasant trot. The stars are sprinkled on the dark, silky sky like diamonds. Romance is in the air! The newlyweds sit close. They take every moment to gaze at one another as the moon provides the light needed for the journey. However, after riding for some miles, things begin to change.

The husband's attention is more on steering the horse. The carriage now veers off the desired path. The wife demands to take control; and conflict erupts. As the two struggle for control of the leather reins, the horse picks up speed and dashes into the woods. A leisurely ride develops into a life-threatening nightmare. When the carriage finally falls over, the couple's internal wounds hurt more than their external bumps and bruises. This imaginative picture illustrates an important fact: couples who choose the love of power over the power of love will only get hurt in the end.

This chapter is dedicated to keeping peace in the marriage. All kinds of things can disturb marital peace. Therefore, we must remain alert and not allow the cares of this world to insidiously seep into our homes. You don't have to go far to have your peace disturbed.

We are living in fearful times. The newscasters perpetuate reports like the world stock market dropping and the country's gas prices rising. People are losing their jobs, homes, and medical assistance. I really could go on with the negative bulletins that bombard our daily lives.

However, by focusing on the negatives we'll never see the positives. We must hang a sign outside the door of our life that reads *Do Not*

Disturb! In essence, we must seek peace. Amazingly, in marriage, anything can disturb your peace.

For example, I do the bulk of the driving whenever Andrea and I travel by car. You would not believe some of the things I must endure. Andrea, from the passenger seat cries, "Slow down!" "Watch out!" "Can you see that?" And here's her personal favorite: "Do you need me to drive?" Unfortunately, these comments have become commonplace in our car. I hear them so often that they are like songs played whenever we take a ride. "Do you need me to drive?" stayed on top of the billboard chart for sixteen weeks straight.

Ironically, whenever Andrea drives, she violates all the driving codes she expects me to uphold. Although it's difficult, I resist the temptation to play songs like "Slow down!" or "Can you see that?" Within recent years I discovered Andrea's need to direct me. She revealed that her peace comes when she is in control.

Many marriages suffer due to control issues. People are often disturbed when they are not in control. If we are to succeed, we will have to find comfort being *under* control not just *in* control. This means giving up the *love of power* in order to discover the *power of love*. Couples must choose the power of love over the love of power to accomplish the marriage mandate: peace.

THE LOVE OF POWER

Those with a love of power need to control everything and everyone. If you are married and possess the love of power, chances are you are unhappy. When couples look to dominate each other, their marriage suffers.

Now, I understand there's nothing like being in control. You gain a sense of confidence and you're able to get things accomplished when you operate with control. Take note, I said when you operate *with* control. This means you can live *under* control without being controlling. You are able to discipline yourself without having to place a demand on others. It is possible to be in control without being a controller.

There are three primary ways controllers try to maintain power over their spouse—intimidation, exploitation, and manipulation.

THE LOVE OF POWER	
Intimidation	To frighten or subdue in order to get one's own way
Exploitation	To utilize or take advantage for one's own purpose
Manipulation	To influence or manage unfairly and unscrupulously for one's own gain

These three strategies are used to acquire power over another. The person who uses these tactics is selfish. Maintaining a healthy marriage means avoiding these destructive tactics at all costs. Resisting the love of power allows you and your spouse to have peace in the relationship.

I can recall when I enlisted in the United States Army. I knew I had to undergo rigorous physical training. Therefore, prior to entering I began a workout regimen. I conditioned my body for whatever physical challenge I would meet.

Upon arriving at boot camp, I discovered something new. Sure, the course was designed to see how much physical training I could endure. Even more, it was designed to see how well I could take commands. All day every day drill sergeants shouted out instructions. Being able to remain under control while under pressure takes the right attitude. The right attitude will produce the right behavior.

Amazingly, as I was able to operate under the control of the drill sergeant's commands, I had more peace. Although I was not controlling the situation, I had confidence in the drill sergeant's experience. This provided a peace throughout the course.

One day a bystander arriving at the airport saw a well-dressed businessman yelling at a porter about the way he was handling his luggage. At every turn the businessman gave the porter orders concerning his job.

The more irate the businessman became, the calmer and more professional the porter appeared. When the abusive man left, the bystander complimented the porter on his restraint. "Oh, it was nothing," said the porter. "You know, that man's going to Miami, but his bags—they're going to Brazil." People who have the love of power and look to usurp authority over others often reap negative consequences.

The Power of Love

A ship was wrecked in a furious storm and the only survivor was a little boy who was swept by the waves onto a rock. He sat there all night long until the next morning when he was spotted and rescued. "Did you tremble while you were on the rock during the night?" someone later asked him. "Yes," said the boy, "I trembled all night—but the rock didn't."

Jesus is that rock we live upon. When we fall upon hard times or our marriage is in a season of darkness, just know that although we may be shaking, our foundation (Jesus) is stable.

Couples who have discovered and operate from the power of love enjoy an enriched and fulfilled marriage. Love is powerful! Through love you learn to express a deep and profound desire to see your spouse succeed. People who enjoy love at this level possess peacefulness. When you have peace ruling your heart you become a peace officer. A peace officer is one who maintains the peace. They come in peace so their spouse may go in peace.

Be forewarned, fear can prohibit peace. Whenever fear tries to grip my heart, I remind myself of the following scripture:

> For God hath not given us the spirit of fear, but of power, and of love, and of a sound mind.
>
> —2 Timothy 1:7, kjv

God has not given us the spirit of fear. His Word forever reminds us of His unfailing love. For that reason, I remind my wife often of my undying love for her. How about you? If you have not told your spouse you love them lately, wait no longer; share your heart.

In the Book of Ruth the Bible tells us about Boaz and Ruth, who reveal the power of love that brings about peace. This couple really loved and supported each other. We see a beautiful love story through their relationship.

Their story begins as Ruth makes the decision to journey to her mother-in-law's place of origin. After the death of her husband, Ruth could have returned to her own people. Nevertheless, (with her future looking grim) she devoted herself to the welfare of Naomi.

Upon arriving in Bethlehem Ruth went to work. She worked faithfully to feed her mother-in-law and herself. This is a beautiful picture of the power of love. Many struggle when it comes to loving their spouse's parents. This struggle can disturb the peace of the marital union. On the other hand, Ruth loved Naomi, and it showed in her service and obedience.

Having God's love in our heart reflects how we treat others. Boaz possessed the love of God. This was evident by how he spoke. Look at how the Scripture reveals him greeting those who worked for him:

> And, behold, Boaz came from Bethlehem, and said unto the reapers, The LORD be with you. And they answered him, The LORD bless thee.
>
> —RUTH 2:4, KJV

Many marriages are void of peace without Jesus, who is the Prince of Peace. Some receive Christ into their life, but they still have not allowed Christ to rule their life. I like to say they are related *to* the Lord, but there's no relationship *with* the Lord. To have a relationship with the Lord, we must saturate our minds in the Word of God.

Boaz was a man with a deep relationship with God. Therefore, when he met Ruth there was a peace in his heart to treat her with kindness. He instructs his servants to allow Ruth to drink of their water and leave grain for her to take home (2:15–16).

Ruth responds to Boaz's kindness with humility.

> Then she fell on her face, and bowed herself to the ground, and said unto him, Why have I found grace in thine eyes, that thou shouldest take knowledge of me, seeing I am a stranger?
>
> —RUTH 2:10, KJV

> Then she said, Let me find favour in thy sight, my lord; for that thou hast comforted me, and for that thou hast

spoken friendly unto thine handmaid, though I be not
like unto one of thine handmaidens.

—RUTH 2:13, KJV

The true beauty of this couple lies in their discovery of the power
of love through complete submission to the lordship of Jesus Christ.
For this reason, Boaz revealed himself a true gentleman and Ruth a
woman of sincere humility. When husbands and wives can operate
in the same spirit of this biblical couple, peace will rule their hearts
and homes. Marital counseling is often needed because peacefulness
is absent in the home.

The power of love caused Boaz to provide safety and security for
Ruth, a stranger in a foreign land. Ruth revealed that she desired Boaz
to be the husband who would love, serve, and protect her. The following scripture shows Boaz's prompt response:

And he said, Blessed be thou of the LORD, my daughter:
for thou hast shewed more kindness in the latter end than
at the beginning, inasmuch as thou followedst not young
men, whether poor or rich. And now, my daughter, fear
not; I will do to thee all that thou requirest: for all the city
of my people doth know that thou art a virtuous woman.

—RUTH 3:10–11, KJV

Boaz claimed Ruth as his wife and the two raised a family in a well-
nurtured environment. Through peace they were able to overcome
many obstacles such as poverty, prejudice, and even in-laws. Like this
couple, we can experience the power of love in our marriage through
peace. No matter what issues you face, peace can calm every storm.

As of late, Andrea does much better. She still twitches and bites her
lip from time to time when I drive. Nevertheless, phrases like "Do
you need me to drive" have been replaced with "Let me know when
you get tired." Her need for control seems to have been replaced with
concern. Either way, I'm just elated our drives are a lot more peaceful.

If peace was made possible in my car, I know it's possible in your
marriage. Just reject the love of power and pursue the power of love.

GENTLENESS

Moving wisely, touching softly, talking
quietly, and thinking kindly.

Unnecessary Roughness

GENTLENESS

Chapter Eight

At the age of nine, a favorite pastime of mine was going to the matinee to see creature movies with my two older brothers and our friends. Our Uncle Richard owned the theater and would allow all us kids to get in free on Saturday afternoons. To our friends we were the kings of the hill (at least on Saturdays).

Every Saturday we were frightened and fascinated by the likes of creatures such as Dracula, the Werewolf, the monster of Dr. Frankenstein, the Mummy; you name it, if there was a creature, Uncle Richard showed them at his theater.

Those days as a child growing up in Philadelphia were special to me. No matter how dull the weekdays went, the guys and I could always look forward to our Saturday group stroll to Uncle Richard's theater. Life was simple back then. You knew exactly who the creatures were. Creatures today are a bit more complicated to detect. The faces that were engraved in my mind as a child and deemed dangerous have changed. Through the years faces like Dracula and the Werewolf have been replaced with faces like Ted Bundy or Jeffrey Dahmer. Now the creatures of the world look normal. Even worse, some have seen danger in the faces that live in their very homes. No longer is the monster on another planet, it could be in another room.

Monsters create havoc and terror; and the last place you expect to find monsters are in a marriage. Let me say, I write this chapter with the utmost sensitivity. My hope is to bring marriages to a place of wholeness and health. Gentleness will keep any marriage healthy. In my last book, *Marriage Matters: Learning to Love like God*, I devoted an entire chapter to kindness. Therefore in this book, rather than discussing the topic of gentleness, we will explore the very antithesis of it.

Before we do, I would like to make clear that gentleness is my focal point. The only reason for going in the other direction is to reveal a harsh reality in marriage when gentleness is not employed.

If nothing else, a marriage should be a place of safety and security. Gentleness makes this possible. My heart truly goes out to anyone who has to endure abuse of any kind. More importantly, God desires for couples to dwell together in harmony and peace.

Domestic violence is not something discussed openly in many environments. It certainly is not a topic you hear often within the Christian community. However, it is with a heavy heart I must report that it happens frequently both in and outside the church.

Through gentleness we have patience to handle our spouse with care. When there is no gentleness in our hearts, it could spell danger in our homes. Gentleness is fundamental in the prevention of spousal abuse.

LOOKING AT THE DARK SIDE

The dark side of marriage is the damage caused to one's emotional, mental, and physical well-being by a marital partner. Comfort, support, and well-being for life shared between the two is the bright side of marriage.

In the Book of Judges, chapter 19, we find a most disturbing account. A man travels to his father-in-law's house to get his wife. After visiting with his father-in-law for days, he journeys back home with his wife. On the way he encounters some disgusting desperados. These criminals sexually abuse his wife. Even worse, after returning home, the husband cuts her into twelve pieces. (See Judges 19:25–29.) This woman was a victim of both sexual and domestic violence. Even more shocking, the culprit of the domestic violence was a man who served the Lord. Unfortunately, domestic violence happens within the family of God.

I'm aware this biblical account is totally extreme and a bit graphic. However, it depicts the dark side of marriage. Marriage is set up by God to provide a place of love, comfort, and support. In order to fulfill this goal, there must be gentleness. God Himself protects His people and entreats them with gentleness.

You protect me with salvation-armor; you hold me up with a firm hand, *caress me with your gentle ways.* You cleared the ground under me so my footing was firm.
—PSALM 18:35–36, THE MESSAGE, EMPHASIS ADDED

God is gentle to us. Therefore, He expects us to be gentle and polite to each other.

Remind the believers…*to be gentle and polite* to all people.
—TITUS 3:1–2, EMPHASIS ADDED

ABUSE PREDICTORS AND LEARNED BEHAVIORS

Spousal abuse can occur for years when the abuser and/or the one abused choose to ignore it is happening. God does not want us to endure or ignore abuse of any kind, especially spousal abuse. Notwithstanding, I need to make a point. Spousal abuse can start off small with belittling each other with words; but if not checked, it can escalate to something big such as verbal threats or physical attacks.

Normally, it's difficult to predict who would be a spousal abuser. However, there are studies that suggest certain causes. Some research lists risk factors for men who abuse women and they are:

- Extensive unemployment

- Users of illicit drugs or abusers of alcohol

- High school dropouts

Still, other research advocates when men experience powerlessness or inadequacy in the areas of *employment, earnings,* or *education* they can become candidates for marriage conflict or violence. These are *predictors not predictions.* Other predictors of abuse are:

- Disregard of spouse's thoughts and feelings

- Withholding affections with cruel intentions

- Giving a spouse the silent treatment

- Ridiculing or insulting a spouse

- Constant yelling at a spouse during discussions

- Prohibiting a spouse from socializing with others

- Damaging property or a spouse's possessions

Whatever the case, we must look at the dark side and not ignore it. Being aware of the signs early allows us to address the problem and possibly avoid physical and emotional harm. Let us examine a destructive cycle.

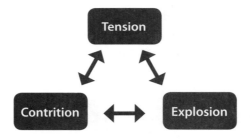

First, there is usually *tension* brought about through stressors. Second, situations escalate and eventually there's an emotional *explosion*. Finally, the one inflicting the pain expresses *contrition* for their destructive actions and promises the event won't happen again.

Usually when a spouse has gone as far as physical abuse, the chances of it recurring are great. This destructive cycle just seems to repeat itself. However, if anyone really repents to God and surrenders their life to the power of the Holy Spirit, freedom from this marital destruction is possible.

It's uncommon to become an abuser overnight. This kind of behavior can be learned or transferred. In many homes, girls are encouraged to share their feelings but are not allowed to show anger. On the other hand, boys are allowed to express anger but are forbidden to express their feelings. In a healthy environment, both must learn to express anger and their feelings in ways that are constructive not destructive.

If children are subjected to the following abuses, a pattern of abuse can possibly be instilled:

TYPES OF ABUSE	
Physical Abuse	To cause bodily injury
Physical Neglect	Lack of food, clothes, shelter or medical attention
Physical Abandonment	Left in house or car alone for long periods of time
Emotional Neglect	Deprived of parent's interest and touch
Verbal Abuse	Being put down, name-calling, or overly criticized
Sexual Abuse	Exposed to inappropriate sexual bonds or behavior
Chaotic Abuse	No stability or peace in the home
Social Abuse	Over protected; lacking interaction with others

CONSIDER THE FACTORS OVER FEELINGS

If you live with a spouse who suffers from *no-gentleness-disorder* (my term), you can do something about it. First of all, pray. Tell God what troubles you and ask Him to change your situation. God is still in the business of answering prayers.

The following scripture reveals how God feels about the afflictions of His children:

> And the LORD said, I have surely seen the affliction of my people which are in Egypt, and have heard their cry by reason of their taskmasters; for I know their sorrows; And I am come down to deliver them out of the hand of the Egyptians.
>
> —EXODUS 3:7–8, KJV

Next, you can go to your spouse and let them know how you feel. Let them know love doesn't inflict hurt. Finally, if your spouse does not listen to your request for relief, you *must* tell someone. Some abusers try to isolate their victims in order to conceal their awful activities. However, you must realize and decide that your life is valuable. Do not allow anyone, especially a spouse, to convince you differently.

A union which depicts spousal abuse to the core is the relationship between Samson and Delilah. This was a relationship doomed from the start. Samson was a sucker for a pretty face. He constantly walked a volatile tightrope in respect to women. He ignored the factors and gave in to his feelings. When we ignore certain factors about our spouse (how they treat us) only because we have feelings for them, this can cause the situation to worsen.

Samson thought Delilah was a woman he could let down his hair with (figuratively and literally) and this would prove to be his downfall. Take note, Samson was not innocent in this botched bond he shared with Delilah. He rested in her lap while spawning one lie after another.

Amazingly, every time Samson would supposedly reveal his weakness, she would call for people to cause him harm. It was obvious Delilah meant him no good. However, Samson didn't wise up, cut his losses, and leave this woman alone. This brings us to the most frequently asked question when it comes to domestic violence: Why doesn't the abused person leave?

There are multiple reasons why a person would stay in a volatile relationship. Some victims of abuse stay hoping their spouse will change. Others are committed to the belief that God hates divorce. Many are embarrassed by the ordeal and try to avoid the proverbial "I-told-you-so" from family and friends. Then there are those who lack economic strength and feel survival without their spouse is impossible.

Allow me to retort: yes, God does hate divorce, but He loves us. I believe with all my heart that God would rather see your marriage end than your life. Anger gets us in trouble. However, pride keeps us there. Please do not allow pride to hold you in an unhealthy union because you are afraid of what others may say. Also, the lack of money should never cause a person to remain in an abusive situation. "With

God all things are possible" (Matt. 19:26). Therefore, if you have to lose everything to save your life, God will restore your losses; just trust and believe He can.

Delilah was able to weaken Samson by playing on his feelings. Eventually, he broke down and collapsed under her control.

> Then Delilah said to him, "How can you say, 'I love you,'
> when you don't even trust me? This is the third time you
> have made a fool of me. You haven't told me the secret of
> your great strength." She kept bothering Samson about his
> secret day after day until he felt he was going to die!
> —JUDGES 16:15–16

Delilah challenged Samson's love for her by saying, "You have made a fool of me." This ploy pulled on Samson's emotions and caused him to become putty in Delilah's hands. Oftentimes victims of abuse are made to feel they caused the mistreatment. Hence, they collapse into their spouse's destructive behavior.

Samson discovered the hard way not to trust his feelings over factors. We can look to him and see what lying in the wrong lap can do. When the factors point to danger, do not allow your feelings to get in the way. Nevertheless, where there is hope, there is help.

HOPE FOR THE HOPELESS

The last thing the devil wants you to know in a domestic violence case is that there is hope of recovery. Of course, there is help for the abused in the local church as well as through government agencies.

Moreover, I want to address the person who has been the abuser. Please do not allow guilt and shame to be your covering. If you really desire to stop hurting the one you love, it's time to come to God with a heart of remorse. If you repent, God can repair.

> *Mercy* and *truth* are met together; righteousness and
> peace have kissed each other.
> —PSALM 85:10, KJV, EMPHASIS ADDED

This scripture conveys that when we come to God with the truth, He will meet us with mercy. Once mercy and truth meet, righteousness and peace will kiss. To be righteous means we are in right standing with God. Through this right standing, our hearts and home will experience peace.

In the Hebrew culture various offerings were presented to God for different reasons. The two I would like to highlight are the burnt offering and the trespass offering.

TYPE	PURPOSE	OFFERING
Burnt Offering	Atonement for sin in general	Unblemished bull, male sheep or goat; male or female dove or pigeon
Trespass Offering	Injured persons compensated for their losses	Unblemished ram

These offerings are fundamental. They reveal God's help in what can seem to be a hopeless situation.

To develop our thought, let's look at a man by the name of Abraham. This man was unable to have children with his wife, Sarah. So, he and his wife agreed that Abraham would have a child with Sarah's bondservant. Well, this course of action (as one would expect) took an ugly turn. Eventually the bondservant and the child were put out of Abraham's house (Gen. 21:9–14).

God needed to keep His covenant with Abraham; but in order for there to be a covenant, Abraham had to present the burnt offering (22:2–3). Normally, Abraham would have a lamb for the burnt offering (vv. 7–8). However, on this occasion God Himself provided a ram (v. 13). Just what makes this ram so significant? As noted above, the ram was used for the trespass not the burnt offering.

In essence, Abraham was prepared to repent for general sin, but God had a specific one in mind. The bondwoman Hagar had been injured emotionally and Abraham had to own up to that before he could go on with God.

> And whosoever lieth carnally with a woman, *that is a bondmaid*, betrothed to an husband, and not at all redeemed, nor freedom given her, she shall be scourged; they shall not be put to death, because she was not free. And he shall bring his *trespass offering* unto the LORD, unto the door of the tabernacle of the congregation, even *a ram* for a trespass offering.
>
> —LEVITICUS 19:20–21, KJV, EMPHASIS ADDED

Abraham fathered a child with this bondwoman that resulted in her becoming homeless. For that injury God Himself provided forgiveness through the *Ram* in the bush.

My friend, if you have been snared by the act of being a physical abuser to your spouse, God has a "Ram in the bush" for you. The Ram's name is Jesus, and He gives hope to the hopeless. Roughness in marriage is really unnecessary. Therefore, if you suffer from *no-gentleness-disorder*, allow God to touch your life and make you meek and mild.

Years after I grew up, I discovered that my Uncle Richard's theater went out of business. I asked him why the theater closed. He said, "People just weren't interested in creature shows anymore." Who knows? Maybe if Uncle Richard would have changed his movies, it would have saved his theater. This I do know, if we are gentle and keep the creatures out of our homes, it can save our marriages.

ADDITIONAL ABUSE INSIGHTS

How do you stop abuse?

- Don't lose your self-esteem
- Admit there is abuse
- Set a standard of limitations and stand by it
- Pray to God for direction

How do you stop abusing?

- Admit you are an abuser

- Recognize the damage you caused

- Don't blame others or your spouse for your problems/actions

- Pray to God for deliverance

When should I stay in the relationship?

- Your spouse has asked for forgiveness, sought professional and spiritual help, and is actively applying counseling instructions

- There is a positive difference to how conflicts are resolved

When do I leave the relationship?

- Your children are being abused in any way

- Spouse continues to threaten you

- There is no respect in the relationship

- You fantasize about killing your spouse

RESPECT

True respect not only sees, it listens to learn.

Let's Make a Deal

RESPECT

Chapter Nine

In February of 2010, Andrea and I joined a caravan of over fifty people from our church and traveled across the globe to Israel. I really do not possess the words to adequately express the wonderful experience we had. I mean, wow! The area we covered in eleven days was remarkable.

We sailed on the Sea of Galilee, prayed in the Garden of Gethsemane, and visited the Western Wall. We were baptized in the Jordan River, took a long walk through Hezekiah's Tunnel, saw the City of David, and gathered mud from the Dead Sea. The entire group sang in the Upper Room, heard stories at Qumran Archaeological Site, and then climbed the Mount of Olives. Our eyes were fastened on the Dome of the Rock and the Golden Gate. We were exposed to so much more. Who could forget of all things traveling on the path of Via Dolorosa? We stood within feet of Golgotha, and finally, we sat in the Garden Tomb.

It was the Holy Land! And I saw practically the entire thing through the lens of my camera. Our assigned tour guide worked tirelessly to help us comprehend and appreciate each site. I can't speak for anyone else, but I was more concerned with recording the moment than respecting the moment. To be quite honest, I saw a lot, but heard very little. True respect not only sees but it listens in order to learn.

Being married should be both challenging and rewarding. Couples can overcome any challenge when the reward of that challenge is great. Marital partners must have a common goal and fight for the same cause. The cause for any couple should be to maintain the health and integrity of their marital union. The essential element to keeping any marriage strong is respect.

Now, I have heard it said, "Respect must be earned!" I tend to disagree. I feel it's better to just give respect rather than make a person earn it. I believe if couples give respect only when they feel their partner has earned it, the marriage may become subject to sickness. On the other hand, if each partner gives respect on the basis of moral obligation and not mere justification, respect will be reciprocated. Respect should be considered *just do*, not *justified*.

It cannot be stated enough, marriage needs respect. Allow the following scriptures to illuminate that point:

> But each one of you must love his wife as he loves himself, and a wife must *respect* her husband.
> —EPHESIANS 5:33, EMPHASIS ADDED

> In the same way, you husbands should live with your wives in an understanding way, since they are weaker than you. But show them *respect*, because God gives them the same blessings he gives you—the grace that gives true life. Do this so that nothing will stop your prayers.
> —1 PETER 3:7, EMPHASIS ADDED

Respect is vital to the life and progression of your marriage. According to Peter, if couples fail to respect each other their prayer life can be hindered. Therefore, it is incumbent to render one another respect.

Andrea and I made a deal: we will respect each other unconditionally. In order to accomplish this, we must provide the Triple-A Treatment. The Triple-A Treatment consist of articulation, attitude, and action.

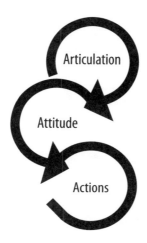

ARTICULATION

When our spouse does something we like, we should tell them. Everyone loves compliments. Life is difficult and at times downright demeaning. In light of this, it would be great to take every opportunity to verbally remind our loved ones how much we appreciate them.

Our compliments energize our spouse. Not to mention, they'll look for opportunities to please us again. There's nothing like a good compliment to make us feel respected.

You might be saying, "Why should I compliment my spouse; he doesn't compliment me?" My friend, if you want your spouse to compliment you, start by planting the seed, then water the seed, and eventually you will see your harvest. Why is it we understand that growing a beautiful garden takes patience and persistence, but we think growing a beautiful marriage or putting one back together should happen overnight?

Begin articulating how you appreciate your husband. Tell your wife how she is admired. Every now and then it is good to write your spouse a love letter. If you're not big on writing, get a card that truly expresses your love and respect. Words are powerful! The right words can make a bitter situation better.

ATTITUDE

An instructor stood at the head of the classroom and for a moment looked each child in the eye. This was the first day of school. To begin the first lesson, the instructor took out a clean white sheet of paper and placed a small black dot in one corner. He then held the paper up high and asked the entire class, "What do you see?" The children yelled out together, "A black dot!" The instructor, while shaking his head, responded, "No one saw the white sheet of paper." He then concluded, "Don't go through life with that attitude."

In marriage we can't afford to major on the minors. The way you see your spouse will determine how you treat your spouse. No one has all their ducks lined up. Anybody who thinks they're perfect has revealed they don't do much thinking. I believe it's safe to say all of us understand we have failures and faults. However, it shouldn't take perfection from our spouse for us to render them respect.

Never allow your spouse's mistakes to cloud your judgment of them. Keep your spouse as the apple of your eye. When your spouse misses the mark, give them credit for aiming for the target. Attitude is critical throughout the course of your union.

Value is associated with respect. When my wife and I were in the process of building our new home, we needed a temporary dwelling place. Some relatives allowed us to stay in their guesthouse rent free. Andrea and I were at a loss for words. We were so grateful for their generous hospitality.

Even though they did not ask us to pay any money, we knew it was only right to respect their property. For this reason, we were extremely careful and extra clean in their house. It would have been gross disrespect for our gracious hosts to return to their home and find it out of sorts. The point is, because we respected the gift, we took care of it.

Again, value is associated with respect. If you see your spouse with value they will respond to you in like manner.

ACTIONS

A man finally went to the doctor after weeks of symptoms. The doctor examined him carefully, and then called the patient's wife into his office.

"Your husband is suffering from a very rare form of anemia. Without treatment, he'll be dead in a few weeks. The good news is it can be treated with proper nutrition.

"You will need to get up early every morning and fix your husband a hot breakfast—pancakes, bacon, and eggs. He'll need a big, home-cooked lunch every day, and then an old-fashioned, meat-and-pota-toes dinner every evening. It would be especially helpful if you could bake frequently—cakes, pies, homemade bread—these are things that will allow your husband to live symptom-free.

"One more thing: his immune system is weak, so it's important that your home be kept spotless at all times. Do you have any questions?" The wife had none. "Do you want to break the news to your husband, or shall I?" asked the doctor.

"I will," the wife replied. She walked into the examination room. The husband, sensing the seriousness of his illness, commented, "It's bad, isn't it?" She nodded, tears welling up in her eyes. "Tell me; what is it?" he asked her. With a sob, she blurted out, "The doctor says you're gonna die."

Couples who have true respect for each other show it in their daily activities. There is a lot to be done in the course of a day. And it can be taxing to care for one another. However, our actions should always reveal the great respect we hold for our spouse.

As a team, couples should sit and talk about the best approach to life's problems. When the plan of attack is discussed, each spouse feels appreciated and respected. A theme that I have adopted in my marriage is that you can look for something to do or you can do what I'm looking for.

The goal should be to do what your spouse is looking for. I know for some this is a huge order to fulfill. Keep in mind, the objective is to help one another not overload each other. I suggest that you and your spouse discover the top three things that the other would like to see happen (if you have not already done so).

I asked my wife, Andrea, "What are the top three things you would like to see me do for you?" Without even looking at me she said, "In what category?" I was afraid to even ask what that statement meant. To think, she has things chronicled in categories for me to do.

Please, don't overwhelm each other. Just think of the top three things you feel would help you the most and ask your spouse to do that. And out of respect for our spouse, let's not just look for something to do; let's really strive to do the top three things our spouse is looking for.

Another way you can respect your spouse is with their time. In other words, show consideration. For instance, your wife is home cooking a meal for the family and you're going to arrive a little late, call and let her know. She prepared that meal anticipating your enjoyment of it. Therefore, don't disrespect the gift through inconsideration.

If you know your husband has an important project or an assignment to complete, don't bombard him with other things that could be addressed later. Unless it absolutely cannot wait, respect his time and see what you can do to relieve some of his stress.

Through respect we desire to give our spouse our best. With this purpose, give your loved one the Triple-A Treatment. Show your respect through your articulation, attitude, and your actions.

Here's an acronym for respect. I believe it will help you in your endeavor to keep your marriage healthy. It certainly has helped mine.

Reach out

Express love

Speak well

Pray for

Exalt each

Cease anger

Take time

If my sabbatical to Israel taught me anything, it taught me to respect the precious moments in my life.

Marriage needs our respect. Let's not become preoccupied with counting the years without truly appreciating what counts. Today you and your spouse should make a deal. Give each other the Triple-A-Treatment. Respect each other through your articulation, attitude, and actions.

GENEROSITY

God's quality living is experienced
through giving.

Love Illustrated

GENEROSITY

Chapter Ten

The film *Schindler's List* chronicled the heroic efforts of a German industrialist named Oscar Schindler. Through his unselfish activities, over a thousand Jews on the trains to Auschwitz concentration camp were saved. Although the film has some graphic and disturbing scenes, the message is profound.

After Schindler learned what was happening at Auschwitz, he began a systematic effort to save as many Jews as he could. He paid for Jews to work in his factory, which was supposed to be a part of the military machine of Germany. On one hand he utilized as many Jews as he could; on the other he secretly sabotaged the ammunition produced in his factory. He entered the war as a wealthy industrialist; by the end of the war, he was basically bankrupt.

As a result of the war, Schindler learned what should be discovered in every marriage. Each of us must be generous if our marriage is to succeed. Many strive to get rather than give. A life replete with huge homes, a few cars, dream vacations, and growing mutual funds is sought after. But more than mutual funds should be mutuality. Marriages flourish not because of huge homes but rather huge hearts.

If we truly live the God-quality life, we must understand we are valued and loved by Him. We are not loved by God because we are valuable; we are valuable because we are loved by Him. For that reason, we must illustrate His love by giving to others. God's quality living is experienced only through giving. As we freely receive we must give.

> I showed you in all things that you should work as I did and help the weak. I taught you to remember the words Jesus said: *"It is more blessed to give than to receive."*
> —ACTS 20:35, EMPHASIS ADDED

Mark it down; when couples are consumed only with hoarding material things, they have a sick marriage. Truly healthy marriages are the ones where you can find God's love operating freely. God's love is never hidden; it is illustrated through generosity.

THE MATTER OF GENEROSITY

In order for us to see the significance of generosity, we must discover something of its origin. The modern English word *generosity* derives from the Latin word *generosus*, which means "of noble birth." Most recorded uses of the term *generous* up to and throughout the sixteenth century reflect an aristocratic sense of belonging to upper class lineage.

Those of the royal families would dispense alms to the less fortunate. By doing so they identified with their wealthy heritage. Our Father owns the cattle upon a thousand hills (Ps. 50:10); Jesus is the King of kings and Lord of lords (1 Tim. 6:15); and most of all, we are joint heirs with Jesus within the royal family of God (Rom. 8:17). Therefore, when the Spirit of God is in you, there will be a desire to give.

As a young man I desired to do great things. I wanted to create some masterpiece or perform a mighty task. I have since retired the notion of the grandiose feats and replaced it with a desire to help my fellow man when I can.

I can recall the very first new vehicle I bought. It was a Dodge Durango. I was so proud to drive that truck. A close friend rejoiced over my fortune and revealed he believed God for the same kind of vehicle.

Some years later I completed my truck payments, kept the truck, and bought another new vehicle. I went from having no car to owning two. I felt as though I was on top of the world. Then that same friend mentioned earlier was in desperate need of transportation. I discussed it with my wife, and we decided to give my truck to him.

I thought nothing could top the feeling I had when I purchased my first new vehicle. However, that feeling was surpassed by the sensation of owning it. Even more exciting was when Andrea and I gave it away.

My friend was elated. He couldn't believe he was receiving the truck as a gift. He thanked Andrea and me for our munificence. In greater manner, he thanked God for the blessing. I listened as he spoke about how God answered his prayers. There is truly no greater experience than when God uses us to bless others. Through the act of generosity, our God was seen. Through giving we identify with our heavenly heritage. The following quote expresses the attitude in which we should give:

> We cannot do great things on this Earth, only small things with great love.
>
> —Mother Teresa[1]

The matter of generosity is the significance in knowing that when you have, you have to give. Through giving we recognize that our lives and the things we possess are not our own. By giving to others we express our allegiance to God our King.

The Message of Generosity

Generous people are liberal. Their lives depict the message "We are free!" If you are in bondage to fear and stinginess, you are not free. However, when you give your time, talents, and treasures and do good works, God will replenish you with plenty more.

> God loves the person who gives happily. And God can give you more blessings than you need. Then you will always have plenty of everything—enough to give to every good work.
>
> —2 Corinthians 9:7–8

First of all, God will *support*.

It shouldn't come as a surprise that God supports His people. As a matter of fact, we find in the very beginning the Earth was without form (Gen. 1:2). Therefore, God restored the form with His firm. The Scriptures record how God made the firmament and called this firmament heaven (vv. 7–8, kjv). The Latin word for *firmament* is *firmamentum*, which literally means to strengthen or support. In essence,

God established and made the first child support, because He provides for His people.

Second, God has *supplies*.

Did you know God doesn't just *have* all that you need? God *is* all you need. When Israel suffered and experienced great lack, God commanded Moses to deliver the message that He would save them. Moses asked God if they ask His name, what name should he give? (Exod. 3:13).

Look at God's response:

> And God said unto Moses, I AM THAT I AM: and he said, Thus shalt thou say unto the children of Israel, I AM hath sent me unto you.
>
> —EXODUS 3:14, KJV

Emphatically God reminds us that He is our supply. When God said tell them I AM, He was revealing His adequate resources to provide what they needed.

Third, God provides *surplus*.

He will always make sure that we have more than enough when we give according to His purpose. When it was time to build a house of worship for God, Moses addressed two kinds of people. He spoke to those who had a *wise* heart (Exod. 35:10, KJV) and those who had a *willing* heart (v. 22, KJV). The people with the wise hearts gave God themselves for the work. The people with the willing hearts gave God their substance for the work. The point is this: they all gave!

As a result of their giving, they had a surplus. Read the following account:

> So Moses sent out orders through the camp: "Men! Women! No more offerings for the building of the Sanctuary!" The people were ordered to stop bringing offerings! There was plenty of material for all the work to be done. *Enough and more than enough.*
>
> —EXODUS 36:6–7, THE MESSAGE, EMPHASIS ADDED

Wow! Isn't that wonderful? The people had to be restrained from bringing their gifts. There was too much stuff! When you get into the heart of giving, you tap into God's overflow. Imagine your marriage being used by God in such a way that you are blessed, others are blessed, and God gets all the praise. When the bondage of fear or stinginess is removed, the message is loud and clear. God supports, He has inexhaustible supplies, and we experience His surplus.

THE MOTIVATION OF GENEROSITY

Generosity is not just giving to someone or something. It is giving without expecting to get anything in return. Many people loan to others and think they're generous; but *loan* implies an expected payback. Financial institutions such as banks and credit unions loan money. And, these institutions expect for their money to be returned with interest.

Two brothers had terrorized a small town for decades. They were unfaithful to their wives, abusive to their children, and dishonest in business. One day the younger brother died unexpectedly.

The surviving brother went to the pastor of the local church. He said, "I want you to conduct my brother's funeral; but it's important to me that during the service you tell everyone my brother was a saint."

"He was far from that," the ministered countered.

The wealthy brother pulled out his checkbook. "Reverend, I'm prepared to give $100,000 to your church. All I'm asking is that you publicly state my brother was a saint."

On the day of the funeral, the pastor began his eulogy: "Everyone here knows the deceased was a wicked man, a womanizer, and a drunk. He terrorized his employees and cheated on his taxes." Then he paused. "But as evil and sinful as this man was, compared to his older brother, he was a saint!"

We should never give with strings attached because somehow that presents a negative outcome. Our motive for giving should flow from a heart to see others do better.

I know of a couple who exemplifies generosity very well. I have known this couple for over twenty years. Their names are Charles and

Martha Smiley. Everyone who has come in contact with this couple has been the better for it.

I know several people who display generosity. Notwithstanding, I know of no couple who demonstrate generosity like this pair. My first impression of Mr. Smiley was a great one. He was so gracious and hospitable. Without understanding why, I began calling him Pop. Pop is a term of endearment that I don't just throw around. It wasn't until later I discovered that everyone (old and young) called him Pop. His wife, Martha, is his perfect counterpart. She is warm and pleasant, funny, and exciting to be around.

They are active and known in the church and community. They are both philanthropist and altruist. They give to causes but it's their love for people that causes them to give. My very first thesis was seventy-eight pages long. Pop Smiley asked if he could read it. I was honored that he asked, but humbled to discover he read it all in one sitting. To think this man would be generous with his time by reading seventy-eight pages of my work was beyond comprehension.

The attention the Smileys give others is astounding. When Martha goes grocery shopping, she buys extra food for those who may drop by their house. This generous duo gives birthday money to countless couples and their children. They possess a wall in their house that displays the degrees and awards of many from the community. I know of people who furthered their education in order to be added to their wall of honor. Imagine that, because of this couple's love and generosity, many have achieved higher learning. These two are truly remarkable. They have positively affected the lives and marriages of so many.

Ralph Waldo Emerson had this view:

> To laugh often and much; to win the respect of intelligent people and the affection of children;... to leave the world a bit better;... to know even one life has breathed easier because you have lived. This is to have succeeded.[2]

This couple's motivation to give stems from the heart of God. When God's heart can be illustrated through our giving, thousands of lives can be made better. The Smileys have never asked for anything in return for their generosity.

True generosity never seeks repayment but it's always repaid. The blessings you receive may not come in the form of money. It can come in the form of a loving family, a healthy life, and just the knowledge that you helped someone else. Whatever the case, when the motivation for giving is pure your marriage and your life will see great rewards.

The Bible records the life of a young woman by the name of Esther. She was practically forced into marriage with an ungodly man. Unlike the Smileys, she and her husband didn't walk in perfect harmony. However, God still blessed Esther with fame and fortune.

The time came when Esther was called upon to risk her own neck for the sake of a nation. Esther didn't have to risk her life. In fact, she was inclined not to do so. It was her cousin who reminded her why God had blessed her to the degree in which He had. Esther's cousin told her that she had been made queen for such a time as this (Esther 4:14). No better words can be spoken. The reason God gives us time, talents, and treasures is because the time will come when others will need them. Esther stepped up and gave what she had. Now the question is, will you?

As for the film *Schindler's List*, Hitler gave the command that at the end of the war all of the Jews were to be murdered. When the Germans surrendered, Schindler met with his workers and declared that at midnight they were all free to go. Millions of Jews died during this time, but not those who worked for Oscar Schindler. The most emotional scene of the film was when Schindler said good-bye to the financial manager of the plant—a Jew and his good and trusted friend. As he embraced his friend, Schindler sobbed and said, "I could have done more!" He looked at his material possessions like his car and his wristwatch and declared, "Why did I save these? I could have bought ten Jews with this. Why didn't I do more?"

Generous people will always feel they should have done more. In your marriage, give all you can to your spouse. Together like Charles and Martha Smiley you both can touch your community, your country, and even the world.

If you are married and you're not quite walking in agreement with your spouse, don't let that stop you from being generous. Like Esther, you can give of yourself and God will see to it that your generosity will touch generations.

LOYALTY

A commitment to go beyond an alliance
to make an allegiance.

I Got Your Back

LOYALTY

Chapter Eleven

Some years ago Andrea and I decided to have our portrait drawn. The artist's God-given gift was on display through the finished product. It captured our better features, and we could hardly wait to hang it for all to see.

First, I purchased a unique frame from a specialty shop. Then we selected what we thought would be the most ideal area in our house to display this work of art. We hung our portrait with pride.

Days later we found our portrait hanging with a major slant. I repositioned it only to discover after some time it was crooked again. This presented a real problem. After investigating I unlocked the mystery of the continued contortion.

The unique frame was heavy and needed more support. I had to locate the stud behind the wall and mount the frame there. Like our portrait, marriage needs not only style, it requires support. This support is loyalty.

If I am loyal to my wife I must become the stud. In other words, I must make my wife feel I have her back. She should be able to face any challenge knowing she has my support.

Couples who support each other through loyalty can count on their marriage remaining healthy. Loyalty means that no matter the circumstances or conflict you can be counted on. It is a commitment to go beyond an alliance and to an allegiance. A loyal soldier doesn't desert his country. A customer who is loyal sticks to their favorite brand. Couples who are loyal to each other are respected and they are friends.

> One of the most important things we give in any friendship is our loyalty, a trait that sometimes seems as though it needs to be placed on an endangered virtues list. Loyalty to family, to country, to community, to one's company—we

93

should not regard these as quaint, outmoded notions. In an age when people are told to "do what feels good" and "do your own thing," the idea of loyalty reminds us that often we should be ready to look past our own needs and put someone or something else first. Loyalty, at bottom, means self-sacrifice, the kind of self-sacrifice that gives solid meaning to relationships.

—William J. Bennett[1]

Again, couples will need to understand the concept of the marital S.T.U.D and apply it to everyday situations. First, we understand that the stud behind the wall is unseen. Therefore, it is not important to stand in front of your spouse. When you have the mentality of the supporter, you allow your spouse to be first. In fact, you desire that your spouse is in front and respected for the same qualities that attracted you to them.

Second, there are qualities that a marital S.T.U.D possesses that will ensure unification within the couple.

Strength—I can carry you.

Trust—I can be counted on.

Unwavering—I can stand still.

Devoted—I can love you.

Strength: I Can Carry You

Strength is vital if the relationship is to last. Unfortunately, we can't always be strong. There will be points in our life when we are weak. However, in marriage we have the unique advantage of having someone there who can carry us when we're unable to do so ourselves.

Two people are better than one, because they get more done by working together. If one falls down, the other can help him up. But it is bad for the person who is alone and falls, because no one is there to help.

—Ecclesiastes 4:9–10

94

My wife and I rely on each other. Sure there are times when we try to take on tasks alone. In fact, there are times when we need to handle situations without the other. In light of this, whenever we need to feel the support of the other, we know it's there. I have Andrea's back and she's behind me encouraging and supporting me to do my best.

There's a couple who inspire Andrea and I in a tremendous way. Greg and Carol are like any couple, they have dreams and desires for their marriage. However, they have experienced a difficulty. Only a few years after marrying, Carol became physically ill. She began losing her vision and eventually had to be transported everywhere by wheelchair. Her physical state seemed to worsen each month until finally she had to be hospitalized.

The past years of their marriage have been spent with Carol residing in the hospital. Greg continues to raise their daughter and, every day as much as he can, he's by his wife's side. In spite of Carol's present condition, she continues to live with high spirits and an earnest expectation to make a full recovery.

Carol is asked often how she is able to maintain her composure and remain confident that her health will return. She credits two sources. First, she gives God the glory for granting her peace in the midst of her storm. Then she gives her husband praise for his love, which is displayed through his loyalty. Rather than complaining, Greg has chosen to carry his wife and daughter through this unfortunate ordeal.

It takes an inner strength that only God can provide to get us through the misfortunes in life.

> But he said to me, "My grace is enough for you. When you are weak, my power is made perfect in you." So I am very happy to brag about my weaknesses. Then Christ's power can live in me. For this reason I am happy when I have weaknesses, insults, hard times, sufferings, and all kinds of troubles for Christ. Because when I am weak, then I am truly strong.
>
> —2 Corinthians 12:9–10

It is good to know that the source of our strength is God. Therefore, when we are called upon to carry our spouse, it is made possible through God carrying us.

TRUST: I CAN BE COUNTED ON

Trust is important and should never be taken for granted. Trust is also a good preventive medicine. Trust can most certainly cause us to live longer healthier lives; because of trust we can live stress free. When the trust level is low, the stress level is high. Take airports for example. Before 9/11 passengers could move through airport checkpoints with ease. Post 9/11 has proven to be more difficult to get through the same checkpoints.

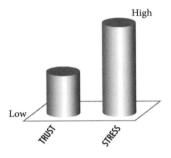

A healthy marriage is determined the same way. When couples are able to trust one another, stress is avoided. As long as couples are truthful with each other, movement within the home and marriage is done with ease. However, once trust has been breached or totally broken, movement within the marriage becomes as difficult as those airport checkpoints.

There are many classifications floating around that help us determine people's personalities, but the most widely accepted is the type A and B personality traits. Let's only focus on the type A person. Those with type A traits are impatient, driven, and easily provoked to frustration. The type A person finds it difficult to trust others to perform any task and therefore perform the task themselves. If not careful they can become distrustful of their mate and allow undo stress to enter into the relationship.

It is imperative that married couples convey and extend trust in each other. If you happen to be a type A personality, do your best to regulate the urge to control your marriage. Trust that your partner is there for your support. Remember, stress will eventually make a mess of you and your marriage. Therefore, remove the stress through trust.

The most important couple in the Bible was Joseph and Mary, the parents of our Lord and Savior Jesus. This couple was given the significant task of raising the Redeemer of humanity. For that reason, having a healthy relationship was of utmost importance.

The very first challenge that Joseph had to face was that of trust. While Joseph and Mary were engaged, Mary became pregnant and Joseph knew he had no sexual relations with her. Therefore, he contemplated not espousing Mary at all (Matt. 1:19). However, an angel spoke to Joseph in a dream concerning his future wife, the expected child, and God's purpose for their life.

At first Joseph was filled with stress, but his stress was soon replaced with trust. Through trust he married this virgin girl and the two of them raised a son like the world has never seen. Supporting through trust allows your spouse to see that you have their back.

UNWAVERING: I CAN STAND STILL

> He that wavereth is like a wave of the sea driven with the wind and tossed. For let not that man think that he shall receive any thing of the Lord.
>
> —JAMES 1:6–7, KJV

Showing loyalty to our spouse means that we do not waver in our commitment to stand with them. Even when our spouse is not measuring up to their role as a husband or wife, we should not be quick to quit the relationship. When you married it should have been for better *and* for worse.

There are too many fair-weather spouses. They are around when the conditions are favorable. In contrast, when the going gets tough; they get going. There needs to be an I-can-yes-I-can! attitude.

One of the best things I did was attend college while married and raising a family. Now, I didn't say it was easy. There were a lot of courses I wanted to drop. There were many assignments I didn't think I could accomplish. Nevertheless, I was committed to succeeding, and my wife learned something that money cannot buy. She learned she didn't marry a quitter.

In some cases, she watched me accomplish my goal through sweat, hard work, and dedication. Consequently, she saw my unwavering determination to succeed. I have that same mentality when it comes to my family and my marriage. There are days when it seems like the bottom will fall out, but my wife and I are unwavering in our resolve. Through this we are stronger and even more committed to supporting each other.

A small boy was among some skaters, obviously a beginner; his frequent falls stirred the pity of a well-meaning spectator. She said, "Little boy, you don't have to stay on the ice and keep falling down. You can come into the stands and watch the other skaters." As the boy got back to his feet he said, "I didn't get new skates to give up with; I got them to learn how with."

Now, shouldn't that be our mentality when it comes to marriage? Sure, there will be days when you don't do or say the right thing. In essence, we all fall in life and we all fall in marriage. However, falling doesn't have to be final. Falling doesn't have to be fatal. And falling doesn't necessarily mean failing. Falling presents a way to learn to do better.

Our spouse needs to know that our loyalty allows for falling. In other words, they should not be afraid to make a mistake. I like to say, "It's better to try and make a mistake than to make the mistake of not trying." As long as your spouse strives to live honest and harmless in their endeavors, your stance and support must be unwavering.

Devoted: I Can Love You

Devotion in marriage is so fundamental. One of the key aspects in marriage is having someone who will love you unconditionally.

Love in its purest form is simply to sacrifice who and what you have for the sake of someone else. Once you're married your primary objective is to be there for your spouse. It's unwise and unhealthy to think along the lines of getting all your needs met. This kind of perpetual thinking only fosters selfishness which ultimately destroys marital unions.

> I have shewed you all things, how that so labouring ye ought to support the weak, and remember the words of the Lord Jesus, how he said, It is more blessed to give than to receive.
>
> —Acts 20:35, kjv

The previous scripture was spoken by the apostle Paul to the leaders of the various churches he established. The point he made was for the leaders to love the people of God and therefore protect them by sacrificing their lives for their sakes. How much more should we love and sacrifice for the spouse we have been entrusted to care for?

Someone might say, "I'll love my spouse when they act lovable." To that I say if you love a person when they're only behaving in a lovable manner, you do not love at all. Love extends beyond behavior and reaches into a person's being. In essence, love sees a person's capabilities and does not discriminate because of their inabilities.

Loyalty at its best is on display through love. Becoming a marital S.T.U.D is vital to keep the life of our marriage strong. It's through strength, trust, unwavering commitment, and devotion that our spouse feels our support and knows that we are loyal.

The portrait that Andrea and I had drawn is hanging straighter than ever. People still come to our house and comment on the beauty of the portrait. Some even say that the expensive frame really accentuates the portrait's uniqueness. Oddly enough, what they don't see is what really makes it all work. The stud behind the wall may not get praise, but it holds all the power.

In my marriage I strive to be that marital S.T.U.D that says to my wife, "Go ahead, look your best; and remember, I got your back."

Through loyalty you can say the same thing and receive the same results of my portrait—praise and, most of all; the presence of each other's support.

COMPASSION

Deep empathy for the suffering of others.

Have a Heart

COMPASSION

Chapter Twelve

Araminta Ross was one of eleven children born to Benjamin and Harriet Green Ross in Dorchester, Maryland. During adolescence, her servitude was rendered to other plantation owners where she was denied an education and beaten brutally for the smallest of infractions. As an enslaved child, young Araminta rebelliously changed her name to Harriet.

She received a beating as an adolescent that stands out the most. It was so severe it caused her to suffer blackout episodes for the remainder of her life. Although she married a freeman, John Tubman in 1844, Harriet was still considered a slave. Three years later, after the threat of being sold into slavery and sent into the Deep South by her husband, she escaped to the North.

As a free woman, one would think she would have lived in the North enjoying her liberated status. Who would have blamed her? After all, she certainly deserved an easier life. However, she did not take the easy life.

Harriet Tubman single-handedly led hundreds of American slaves to freedom along organized units known as the Underground Railroad. With slave scouts looking to kill her at every turn and despite the threat of losing her own life, she returned to the South at least nineteen times with one purpose—to free others. Tubman personally led more than three hundred men, women, and children to the North and Canada.

Nicknamed the Moses of her people, she also served as a nurse, scout, and spy for the Union Army during the Civil War. In her final years she championed the rights of the elderly and poor.[1]

Just what caused a person who had been through so much suffering to give of herself and even jeopardize her life for the sake of others? I can only think of one word—compassion.

Marriages are not filled with sunny days. There are times when storms come crashing down on the union. There will be times when your partner will need something from you that only you are equipped to give. That something is compassion.

Marriage may start off with passion. Notwithstanding, passion alone will not keep the marriage healthy. There will inevitably come times when passion must give way to compassion. Sure, having passionate flames in your marriage is exciting. Nevertheless, what should we do when the flames become a flicker? What's to be done when a healthy union experiences hurt? At this point it's time to have a heart.

Consider the heart of Jesus:

> He will not break a crushed blade of grass or put out even
> a weak flame.
>
> —MATTHEW 12:20

Compassion compels us to go the extra mile. It causes us not to judge critically. Through compassion we look to meet the needs of the suffering, especially those of our spouse. Compassion converts a flicker to flames.

I conduct marital counseling for many. The common thread missing in dysfunctional marriages is compassion. I usually hear how difficult it is to care for someone who is mean or hard to live with. Having these people in mind, I want to impart the ABCs of compassion. These three simple steps can place you in compassion's neighborhood.

Announce your presence.

Bring what's needed.

Comfort and console.

ANNOUNCE YOUR PRESENCE

The last thing anyone needs to feel when going through an ordeal is alone. It is damaging and demeaning when a person is not at their best and their spouse says, "I can do badly all by myself." This kind of negative statement fosters the notion, "I brought you in my life to make it better not worse." Let me say that our spouse should be our helpmeet not our help. Therefore, they should not be made to feel they alone provide our security. Only God should have that role. He is a present help in our times of need (Ps. 46:1).

However, we should announce to our spouse we are here to help relieve their burden. It is amazing how just knowing your spouse cares can help alleviate pressure. Whenever I am sick it's nice to know my wife is by my side when I need her. Likewise, it is imperative for us to announce that we are there when needed.

The uniqueness of compassion is it moves us from sympathy to empathy. You can sympathize with a person's plight and never feel what they're going through. In contrast, when you empathize with another, you somehow feel their pain. By empathizing you "weep with them that weep" (Rom. 12:15, KJV).

Jesus knew firsthand how to become acquainted with the pain of others. Consider the following scriptures:

> There was nothing attractive about him, nothing to cause us to take a second look. He was looked down on and passed over, a man who suffered, *who knew pain firsthand.* One look at him and people turned away. We looked down on him, thought he was scum. But fact is, it was *our* pains he carried—*our* disfigurements, all the things wrong with *us.* We thought he brought it on himself, that God was punishing him for his own failures. But it was our sins that did that to him, that ripped and tore and crushed him—*our* sins!
> —Isaiah 53:2–5, The Message, emphasis added

Jesus being acquainted with the suffering of humanity announced His presence to save and set free the broken, burdened, and bruised.

> God's Spirit is on me; he's chosen me to preach the Message of good news to the poor, Sent me to *announce* pardon to prisoners and recovery of sight to blind, To

set the burdened and battered free, to *announce*, "This is God's year to act!"

—Luke 4:18–19, The Message, emphasis added

When you walk a mile in your spouse's shoes, you are more appreciative of their struggles. You will also feel the pain of their sore feet. Announcing your presence to your spouse gives them comfort; however, actions speak louder than words.

Bring What's Needed

Announcing our presence with a promptness to help is just the beginning. True compassion causes us to investigate what's actually needed.

When my wife became ill, I wanted to let her know she was loved and appreciated. Therefore, I brought her flowers. Andrea accepted the flowers while obviously still in a lot of pain. I asked if I could do anything to ease her suffering. After thanking me for the flowers, she vehemently requested I bring her some medication. It was then I discovered the flowers were nice, but they weren't needed.

In order to bring what is needed in any situation, we must take the time to investigate the matter. In marriage, we must listen to our spouse. It's not enough to be efficient, we must be effective. Efficiency means we are busy doing what we think will ameliorate the situation. However, when we are effective we take the necessary time to discover what is needed. Then we bring exactly what's necessary to correct the condition. Being effective in marriage takes love.

The following scriptures amplify my point:

> If I gave everything I have to the poor and even sacrificed my body, I could boast about it; but if I didn't love others, I would have gained nothing.
>
> —1 Corinthians 13:3, nlt

> Keep yourselves in the love of God, looking for the mercy of our Lord Jesus Christ unto eternal life. And of some *have compassion*, making a difference.
>
> —Jude 21–22, kjv, emphasis added

Have you ever gone to the hospital sick only to leave feeling worse? I must admit the previous question is a non sequitur. Some are given the wrong prescription for their illness. In some cases this can prove to be fatal.

Likewise, our spouse deserves our attention to detail. When we love them, we are there to care. Also, we are there to bring what they need, not just what is nice.

Jesus, filled with compassion, recognized people's needs and attended to them.

> In those days the multitude being very great, and having nothing to eat, Jesus called his disciples unto him, and saith unto them, I have compassion on the multitude, because they have now been with me three days, and have nothing to eat: And if I send them away fasting to their own houses, they will faint by the way: for divers of them came from far.
>
> —MARK 8:1–3, KJV

Again, Jesus recognized the people's need through compassion and fed them. How much more through compassion are we required to meet the needs of others? Even more, what about the needs of our spouse?

COMFORT AND CONSOLE

The most important thing to remember about comfort is that it's reserved for those in pain. Therefore, we should never make our spouse feel they are a burden to us. God comforts us in our time of trouble and He expects us to do the same for others.

> Praise be to the God and Father of our Lord Jesus Christ. God is the Father who is full of mercy and all comfort. He comforts us every time we have trouble, so when others have trouble, we can comfort them with the same comfort God gives us.
>
> —2 CORINTHIANS 1:3–4

The great thing about the previous scripture is that we are to comfort others and our spouse with the same comfort God gives us. Therefore, if God doesn't make us feel bad when we are not doing well, we should not make others feel bad.

It's nothing worse than feeling down and having someone say, "Quit your bellyaching!" Okay, we may not hear that too often, but how about this one: "It's not that bad; you'll be alright." No matter how you cut it, having someone tell you that what you feel or what you're going through isn't bad is just down right mean.

God's friend by the name of Job had the kind of comforters who make drill sergeants look like caring counselors. They came to Job in his worse condition and rather than comfort they began hurling accusations. I don't know about you, but I can't stand it when I don't feel well and people start 100 questions. Did you wear a coat? Did you eat the right foods? Was it something you said? Was it something you didn't say?

Like Job, to those kinds of comforters I say phooey. Instead of comfort they make you feel you're being interrogated. Job said it best, they are "miserable comforters" (Job 16:2, KJV). However, God has called us not to misery but to ministry.

> We must become successful comforters by being present while others weep, by sharing a shoulder for others to lean on, and by being a reliable and careful listener. We must be dependable and trustworthy with the thoughts that are shared with us and avoid giving hasty answers or worn-out clichés to those who grieve. Grieving people need safety of friends who hold them up rather than hold them accountable for what they express in anger and frustration. Yes, there is the great opportunity for us to be channels of mercy and comfort in the name of our Lord.
>
> —Charles Stanley[2]

The Book of Proverbs records:

> A man hath joy by the answer of his mouth: and a word
> spoken in due season, how good is it!
>
> —PROVERBS 15:23, KJV

Start speaking the right words to your spouse and about your marriage. If your spouse is struggling with a disease or disorder of any kind, be there to help them get through the pain.

The Bible shares with us the story of a woman named Abigail (1 Sam. 25). She was married to Nabal, a very mean man who severely offended King David. Consequently, David threatened to kill Nabal and every man who lived within his house.

Although Nabal was a mingy fool (v. 25), Abigail had empathy for him. When she heard her foolish husband had insulted David, she immediately put the ABCs of compassion into action. She didn't merely send servants; she announced her presence to David by meeting him on the way (v. 20). She brought what was needed and appeased David's wrath (v. 18). Finally, she comforted David with encouraging words and advised him not to act rashly (vv. 24–31).

Through her compassion Nabal's life was spared for the moment. More importantly, Abigail's compassion was reciprocated by David and the two were eventually wedded. When you operate within the ABCs of compassion the rewards can be immeasurable.

Through compassion Harriet Tubman's life touched the lives of so many. In fact, her compassion granted countless people a life of freedom and liberty. Like Tubman, you may touch the lives of many; but with compassion you are sure to touch the lives of those who are around you now.

Remember when your loved one is hurting, use the fundamental concepts of announcing your presence, bringing only what's needed, and comforting them with consoling words. By doing this, your marriage will remain healthy and saturated with love.

DISCRETION

Having prudence under pressure.

Keep a Lid on It

DISCRETION

Chapter Thirteen

The Hoover Dam is one of America's Seven Modern Engineering Wonders. It stands at Black Canyon where Nevada and Arizona meet. Earlier in American history the unchecked Colorado River poured wildly, thus destroying farmlands, homes, and cities. The settlers were at the mercy of its raging torrents.

Something had to be done if lands and livestock were to be saved. In 1928 Congress passed the Boulder Canyon Project Act to authorize construction of the dam. In 1930 President Herbert Hoover signed the bill to begin the work.

The dam was constructed by initially placing dynamite within the walls of Black Canyon for two years. A 135-feet chasm was dug below the river to reach the dam's foundation. Earth, rock, and sand were excavated. The same rock and gravel was then mixed with concrete meeting rigid specifications for the dam's structure.

On May 29, 1935, two years after they had begun pouring the initial concrete, the last concrete was placed in Hoover Dam making it a total of 3¼ million cubic yards. The dam's full height is 726 feet, far above the crest of any other dam yet built by man. It stood complete and effective. Hoover Dam had conquered the Colorado River.[1]

Marriages have been unhealthy and hindered because of the lack of prudence under pressure. And, in some cases, someone leaked private information. Situations that are deemed personal have been made public by a spouse whose tongue caused as much damage as the untamed Colorado River.

There are times in your marriage when discretion is needed. Your marriage is a sacred unity where you and your spouse should feel safe and secure. The sanctity and security of the union is damaged when discretion is violated.

Prudence under Pressure

Have you ever heard the saying: If you can't stand the heat get out of the kitchen? Well, let me tell you, marriage is one big kitchen. The kitchen is one of the most dangerous places in the house. Sharp knives are kept there, and fire is regularly operated there, too.

Operating within the kitchen without getting hurt takes discretion. *Discretion* in its simplest definition means action with caution. Another way to see discretion is to have an understanding of your present situation and surroundings.

If we are to be successful in our marital endeavors, we will need understanding—and a lot of it! Marriage, by and large, presents pressure. Without discretion operating in our lives, we can succumb to pitfalls that are ahead. Decisions concerning our families, finances, and future take discretion.

Discretion connotes prudence. Therefore, we must ascertain the meaning of prudence accurately. Prudence simply means being careful to avoid undesired consequences. Many people take action before thinking a matter through. This is not discretion. Then, there are those who can think a matter through under the most extreme pressures. These are people who possess discretion and will avoid undesired results if it's possible to do so.

Even in our giving to others discretion is important:

> When you do something for someone else, don't call attention to yourself. You've seen them in action, I'm sure—"playactors" I call them—treating prayer meeting and street corner alike as a stage, acting compassionate as long as someone is watching, playing to the crowds. They get applause, true, but that's all they get. When you help someone out, don't think about how it looks. Just do it— quietly and unobtrusively. That is the way your God, who conceived you in love, working behind the scenes, helps you out.
>
> —Matthew 6:2–4, The Message

Again, having the ability to display discretion is paramount. In light of this, how does one receive discretion? Can the ability to perform prudence under pressure be developed into a person? If so, we must discover how.

It's interesting to note that in order for the dam to be erected and stand as the great wonder we see today, dynamite was used. So it is when developing the character of discretion. We must be able to retain information that if mishandled could cause damage or worse— destroy lives.

Both people and problems will cross our paths. If the two happen to be negative it can cause our hearts to harden. The negative situations in our life can form rocks in our inner beings. In the same way the dam was built by rocks, we must use the rocks in our lives to develop us.

We can either use the rocks to fortify a foundation within us or we can allow them to become our downfall. There will be times in our marriages when something is said or done that can cause rocks to form. For that reason, we must handle the rocks, not hold them. When we handle the rocks they are used to our advantage, but holding them and harboring ill toward our spouse places us at a disadvantage.

Take the life of Joseph. He was sold into slavery by his own brothers. He was sold to the captain of Pharaoh's guards. Afterwards, he was wrongfully imprisoned. Through tragedy after tragedy Joseph was not broken but the character of discretion was built within him. The hard knocks in life didn't give Joseph a hard heart; but it created a toughness to endure.

> Moreover He called for a famine upon the land [of Egypt]; He cut off every source of bread. He sent a man before them, even Joseph, who was sold for a servant. His feet they hurt with fetters, he was laid in chains of iron *and his soul entered into the iron.*
> —PSALM 105:16–18, AMP, EMPHASIS ADDED

Joseph was a man who allowed his soul to go into those things that were difficult. Even still, he never allowed the difficulties to enter into him. When Egypt faced a prodigious crisis, they needed a man equipped to handle it. Who better than Joseph? He had faced great opposition himself.

Look at what the Pharaoh had to say concerning Joseph's character, which qualified him for the enormous task:

> And Pharaoh said unto his servants, Can we find such a one as this, a man in whom the Spirit of God is? And Pharaoh said unto Joseph, Forasmuch as God hath shewed thee all this, there is none so *discreet* and wise as thou art: Thou shall be over my house, and according unto thy word shall all my people be ruled: only in the throne will I be greater than thou.
> —GENESIS 41:38–40, KJV, EMPHASIS ADDED

According to the Pharaoh's personal observation, Joseph was a wise man who exercised discretion. Therefore, he was qualified and promoted to the second highest position in the land.

How can a man who has been through so many traumas be this strong? We gain this insight through the testimony of Joseph.

> You meant to hurt me, but God turned your evil into good to save the lives of many people, which is being done.
> —GENESIS 50:20

Like the Hoover Dam and Joseph, our discretion will save the lives of many. We may not save an entire country, but we can start with those on our corner. Through discretion we can save those in our homes. This is possible only if we can handle the rocks in our lives and operate with prudence under pressure.

Consider the following scriptures before moving on:

> When wisdom entereth into thine heart, and knowledge is pleasant unto thy soul; Discretion shall preserve thee, understanding shall keep thee.
> —PROVERBS 2:10–11, KJV

These scriptures convey that through discretion we preserve what we have. When something is preserved it is given new life or at least the life it has is extended.

The Bible also tells us that David, in the face of opposition with King Saul, behaved himself wisely (1 Sam. 18:5). In fact, the Word of God reveals that Saul, although he was king, feared David because of David's discretion (v. 15).

When we can behave in a manner of discretion, we'll do what's proper and appropriate. By discretion all problems, people, and pressure will subside. Through discretion what was once a blaze will be reduced to a simmer and eventually a nonfactor.

DISCRETION WITHOUT DECEPTION

In a healthy marriage couples discuss events that shape their world. However, there are cases when discretion is needed between the spouses. For instance, in my profession as a counselor, I must keep information entrusted to my care confidential. Such cases are few, but when discretion is needed it's important that it is upheld.

Subsequently, there are times when discretion can become quite detrimental to the marriage. For instance, Donald and Dianne sent their daughter, Lisa, to college. Donald was always quite strict about Lisa's friends and her activities. Consequently, when Lisa arrived at college she was thrilled because of her liberties.

Unfortunately, Lisa abused those liberties and eventually became pregnant. When she returned home after her first semester of school, she told her mother of her condition. She asked her mother not to mention the matter to her father because she feared being put out.

Dianne contacted me and asked what she should do. I informed her that discretion by deception is not an option. I further explained that she had a responsibility to her husband not to withhold information like this. This matter concerned Donald as much as it did Dianne. By withholding it, the damage could be irreparable.

Dianne heeded my instructions. At first the situation was bad. However, cooler heads prevailed. Lisa had the child and went on to receive her degree in science.

Withholding anything from your spouse that directly affects them is not being discreet; that is being deceptive. Remember, it is Satan who operates in the dark and seeks to take advantage of our ignorance. Therefore, through discretion be forthright with your spouse and witness the positive growth in your marriage.

> We can easily forgive a child who is afraid of the dark; the
> real tragedy of life is when men are afraid of the light.
> —PLATO[2]

It is when we are open and honest with our spouse that we can receive the true blessings of our marital union. Operating in the light is best. I've heard it expressed that as long as you tell the truth you never have to worry about forgetting what you said.

Isaac and Rebecca represent the danger of deception.

Rebecca was having a complicated pregnancy. Therefore, her heart went to God for some answers. She received a prophetic word from the Lord concerning the twins in her womb, who had already begun to struggle with each other. She was told she had two nations within her. Also, the elder child would someday serve the younger child (Gen. 25:22–23). After receiving this divine news, nowhere do you find Rebecca sharing the prophetic word with her husband.

This couple had their favorites when it came to their sons. Isaac loved Esau, the eldest, and Rebecca loved Jacob, the youngest (v. 28). Isaac and Rebecca's communication suffered. As a result of this, I believe they clung to a child to replace the lost companionship between each other. Displayed parental favoritism is never good for anyone.

One parent overindulges the child while the other parent is hard and critical. Sooner or later the child begins to disrespect the parent who overindulges and despises the parent who criticizes. Through this process the child eventually learns to hurt others in order to get what they want. This is what Jacob did when he stole his brother Esau's birthright (27:18–30).

When we conceal our thoughts and feelings toward our spouse or others in the name of discretion, it could actually be deception. Instead of the results being helpful, it can cause harm. Truthfulness is essential if our marriage is going to remain healthy and thriving.

Allow me the leeway to share a story about deception. Some fishing buddies placed a friendly wager to see who could catch the biggest fish over the weekend. One of the guys went to the neighborhood meat market. He found four of the largest fish in the place and yelled to the butcher, "Toss these big ones to me!"

The butcher replied, "Wouldn't you prefer I wrap and hand them to you in a bag?" The guy explained, "My fishing buddies and I made a bet. And when they ask, I want to tell them I caught these huge fish."

In marriage honesty is not the *best* policy, it's the *only* policy.

We must not withhold vital information about the affairs that affect our lives or our spouse. Withholding information like finances or the daily activities within the family through dishonesty can ruin the relationship altogether.

The apostles Peter and Paul encouraged us about the importance of communicating in the light of honesty:

> So clean house! Make a clean sweep of malice and pretense, envy and hurtful talk. You've had a taste of God. Now, like infants at the breast, drink deep of God's pure kindness. Then you'll grow up mature and whole in God.
> —1 PETER 2:1–3, THE MESSAGE

> God wants us to grow up, to know the whole truth and tell it in love—like Christ in everything. We take our lead from Christ, who is the source of everything we do. He keeps us in step with each other. His very breath and blood flow through us, nourishing us so that we will grow up healthy in God, robust in love.
> —EPHESIANS 4:14–16, THE MESSAGE

In our society discretion has become a dying concept. With social networks like MySpace, Facebook, and more recently Twitter, people are divulging personal information all the time (in many cases too much information). I have personally seen these social networks ruin good relationships. Now, I don't wish to purport the networks themselves promote evil, but there is the potential for great harm.

Another social trend that has ripped through the fabric of America is the advent of reality TV shows. The shows allow people to go on national television to air out their dirty laundry. People with discretion would never participate in such nonsense. Marriage or any relationship should have some value and therefore be protected from public scrutiny and possible humiliation. People who participate in these kinds of programs have only considered the money to be made by them. Money in many cases is a short-term goal. Choosing a short-term goal without considering the long-term effects is not exercising discretion.

The Hoover Dam conquered the Colorado River because of its ability to withstand the pressure. Massive generators at the Hoover Dam power the surrounding states of Nevada, Arizona, and California. The dam has fulfilled the hopes and expectations of those who envisioned its great possibilities. The Colorado River that once destroyed farmlands, homes, and cities now serves them.

Like the Hoover Dam we can harness the pressures of life and make them work toward our good. Through discretion, not deception, our marriage will grow and our families will do better.

> For his God doth instruct him to discretion, and doth teach him.
> —ISAIAH 28:26, KJV

Through God's teachings and His instructions, we are able to remain fortified in our marriage. Most of all, remember; through discretion our marriages can withstand anything.

RESILIENCE

The ability to endure and become new.

Get Over "It!"

RESILIENCE

Chapter Fourteen

John Roosevelt, who was affectionately known as Jackie Robinson, was a great pioneer in American Major League Baseball. Unless you are in the natal stage of life or from an entirely different planet, you have heard of Jackie Robinson.

Often overlooked is the fact that Jackie Robinson served his country as a commissioned officer in the U.S. Army in 1943. He served in the military when racism was promoted and discrimination was provoked. This background would later prove to be a foundation and mental fortitude for his major league career.

Many who followed the American Negro League (for which Robinson had his major league beginning) questioned why he was selected to be the first black to break through the National League's glass ceiling. Many felt he was far from being the best player among his black contemporaries. Invariably, it was to be understood that Robinson was not selected because he was the best player in the Negro League; he was the best suited for the task which awaited him at the next level.

Robinson was chosen to be the first black man to play in the National League for many reasons. Albeit, I believe one reason trumped them all. He was believed and later proven to possess the character that would sustain his career and jumpstart others. Jackie Robinson possessed the spirit of resilience.

Robinson displayed resilience in the face of racism. Although he played the game of baseball, for Robinson it was more than a game. He discovered many hurdles in his National League career. Through verbal attacks, offences, and opposition, Robinson learned and leaned on this truth—when faced with a hurdle, you must "get over it."

Many marriages are torn apart at the seams for lack of resilience.

Having resilience is vital to the life of marriage. Resilience allows the latitude to offend without the union being jeopardized.

Just about everyone can agree life is hard. When faced with adversity, especially in our marriages, we can be quick to throw in the towel and give up. It's no mystery marriage can become quite difficult. However, we must never lose sight of the fact that God is honored through marriage. The Bible reveals that "marriage is honourable" (Heb. 13:4, KJV).

The devil is well aware that we honor God through our unions. Therefore, he does whatever it takes to put us at odds. Nevertheless, the scripture admonishes us to submit ourselves to God and resist the devil (James 4:7). Unfortunately, we find ourselves submitting to the devil (or at least his ways) and resisting God's way.

As long as we are living in this world, we will be confronted with certain challenges. Jesus spoke of the challenges we would face. He called them tribulations (John 16:33). The term *tribulation* is an interesting one. It speaks of trouble, but it's trouble multiplied three times. No matter our ethnicity or cultural background, we all face challenges at one point or another. Whatever the hurdle before you, it comes under one of these three categories—problems, pain, or people.

Let's consider a couple, Job and his wife, who had to endure problems, pain, and negative people.

GETTING OVER PROBLEMS

The most irritating thing about problems is they come unannounced. You can never be prepared for a problem. If you could, it would no longer be considered a problem. This was the case with Job. All of his problems happened the same day.

One day Job and his wife enjoyed success in every area of life. They were happily wedded and wealthy. They were blessed to have seven sons, three daughters, and many servants. The animals and land they owned were enough to start their own zoo. They were paragons of spiritual living and pillars in their community.

Then suddenly it happened! In one day Job lost it all. His health and happy home, his posterity and prosperity were snatched in a matter of hours (Job 1:13–18). This couple was faced with a severe problem.

What should couples do when they are faced with a crisis? Is this a time to fall to pieces or pull the marital union apart? The answer is emphatically No! First of all, couples should remain calm and understand the "Answer" to the problem is always near. For the child of God the answer is *Jesus.*

If asked if 4+4 is a mathematical problem, you would most likely give the answer yes. If asked for the answer to 4+4, you would more than likely answer 8. If this is the case, we must conclude that 4+4 is not a mathematical problem for you. It would be considered a mathematical equation but not a problem. You see, a problem is only a problem when you do not have the answer. The child of God should never see problems the way the world sees them because we have the "Answer" to every problem. His name is *Jesus!*

Jesus is the solution to every problem we will ever face. Look at Job's response to the trouble that hit him:

> Then he bowed down to the ground to worship God. He said: "I was naked when I was born, and I will be naked when I die. The LORD gave these things to me, and he has taken them away. Praise the name of the LORD. *In all this Job did not sin or blame God."*
>
> —JOB 1:20–22, EMPHASIS ADDED

Job did not understand why this great tragedy had befallen his household. He was totally mystified about the Master's (God's) plan. Nevertheless, Job never lost His devotion to God. Therefore, his connection to his wife remained intact.

Many couples falter and fold under pressure and feel they're being punished or unjustly attacked. In these times, understand that God never promised prevention from problems but He does promise protection through them. Again, Jesus warned us that in this world we would encounter trouble (John 16:33).

There will be no prevention from trouble. Trouble is coming! However, God will protect you. God promises, "No weapon that is formed against thee shall prosper" (Isa. 54:17, KJV). Weapons formed against your family, finances, or your future will not succeed as long as you keep your faith in God.

It is absolutely important to remember when problems occur, do not blame God. The scripture reveals that Job did not sin or blame God in his trial.

People traveled across the country to catch the act of a well renowned Bengal tiger tamer. One evening, this tamer was performing his tiger show without a cage. The people were amazed at how the Bengal tigers responded to the crack of the whip and the tamer's commands.

Suddenly, the lights went off beneath the tent where the tamer performed. The place was completely dark. The people knew the tigers were not restricted to a cage. Therefore, they panicked. The tamer sensed the fear of the crowd and immediately instructed everyone to be still and remain seated.

Without missing a beat, the tamer (who could not see a thing) continued to command the tigers and crack the whip. Moments later, the lights beneath the tent were restored. By now, the people thought the light failure was a part of the act.

Afterwards, the tamer was interviewed by the local press. They asked him if he had foreknowledge about the lights going off. He responded, "No!" He was then asked if being in the dark with the tigers made him uncomfortable. The tamer admitted he was horrified.

He further explained that Bengal tigers see perfectly in the dark as well as in the light. In essence, the tigers never knew the lights went off. However, had they sensed the fear of the crowd, everything would have gone awry. Therefore, the tamer calmed the crowd, and continued cracking the whip and speaking with authority. The tigers never knew the difference.

My friend, when problems confront your marriage—when the lights go out—continue speaking God's Word. The devil won't know what to do.

In the middle of every difficulty lies opportunity.
—Albert Einstein[1]

GETTING OVER PAIN

> So Satan left the LORD's presence. He put *painful* sores on
> Job's body, from the top of his head to the soles of his feet.
> Job took a piece of broken pottery to scrape himself, and
> he sat in ashes in misery.
>
> —JOB 2:7–8, EMPHASIS ADDED

Out of the frying pan into the fire was a term Job became acquainted
with first hand. He had lost all he owned. The only thing that out-
weighed his personal loss was the excruciating pain that engulfed his
body. Mentally he went from harmony to agony. Emotionally he went
from wow to woe. Physically he went from power to pain, and from
plus to pus (a bit much huh?).

Every marriage will experience the passage of pain. Whether it
is physical, emotional, financial, sexual, etc., every marriage will be
tested. I heard it said that it's through pain we realize we're still alive.

Take into account the following verse of scripture:

> That I may know him in the power of his resurrection, and
> the fellowship of his *sufferings*, being made conformable
> unto his death.
>
> —PHILIPPIANS 3:10, KJV, EMPHASIS ADDED

In the aforementioned scripture Paul expressed his desired
amalgamation with the Lord. First, it's through the power of His
resurrection. Who wouldn't want to know God's power? However,
don't miss it! Paul said, "The power of his resurrection." In order
for something to be resurrected, it must first experience death. This
brings us to the fellowship of His sufferings.

If you married with the notion that there would never be any pain,
you were naive. There's no real fellowship with Christ without having
your own cross to carry. Make no mistake, the cross stood for shame
and pain. Through Jesus it became a symbol of mercy and grace.

Real marital fellowship involves coming to the cross—when you
cross one another. In other words, you will offend each other. However,
you must let go of the offence in order to go on.

Unfortunately, many marriages fail because couples are not just looking for a painless marriage, they are seeking one that is pain free. Let me tell you, a pain-free marriage is like the Loch Ness Monster, it doesn't exist.

Paul finishes his thought in the scripture by saying he wants to be made conformable unto Jesus' death. This desire contradicts the notion of pain free. To be pain free is to be comfortable. Paul did not say he wanted to be comfortable, but rather conformable. Being made conformable to Jesus is corresponding in form, nature, and Christ's character.

The difference between a piece of coal and a diamond is extreme pressure. Many stand in a coal stage of marriage with diamond desires. If you will allow your marriage to pass through pain, those desired diamonds will become a reality.

GETTING OVER PEOPLE

> Job's wife said to him, "Why are you trying to stay innocent? Curse God and die!" Job answered, "You are talking like a foolish woman."
>
> —JOB 2:9–10

If facing problems and pain in marriage is not enough, take a crack at facing negative people. Confronting negative people is difficult because they often present problems and pain.

Job and his wife had to figure out how to cope with the sudden monsoon of destruction that had devastated their life. Mrs. Job became frustrated and directed her negativity toward her husband. Out of anger, she wished him dead. Out of disappointment, Job likened her to a foolish woman.

How often do you find yourself discouraged and in despair and instead of attacking the problem, you're attacking your spouse. Let's say a person loses their job. They come home disappointed and unsure of the future.

At first their spouse may be very supportive. However, if the jobless spouse doesn't find work soon, the working spouse may accuse them of being inconsiderate. Even worse, the working spouse may claim the other one is lazy and doesn't appreciate the sacrifices that are being made to keep the household together. This is attacking the person and not the problem.

Job felt he was being unjustly attacked by his wife and his friends. The following scriptures reveal Job's thoughts concerning his friends' company in his time of need.

> *You are all painful comforters!* Will your long-winded speeches never end? What makes you keep arguing?
> —JOB 16:2–3, EMPHASIS ADDED

I certainly understand what it's like to be attacked by others. I even mistook other's good intentions as bad actions and, as much as I hate to admit it, I have attacked others myself. There is a natural proclivity to defend yourself. However, more emphasis should be placed on mending and not defending.

> Don't hit back; discover beauty in everyone. If you've got it in you, get along with everybody. Don't insist on getting even; that's not for you to do. "I'll do the judging," says God. "I'll take care of it."
> —ROMANS 12:18, THE MESSAGE

The plan of the devil is to discourage and ultimately destroy every marriage. The enemy only has the authority over your marriage and over your life if you give it to him. When Paul said, "I fought a good fight" (2 Tim. 4:7, KJV), he wasn't speaking of fighting with a spouse, friend, or a neighbor. Paul was referring to the fight of faith he used against the devil. The problems we encounter with others are designed by the devil to discourage us and cause us to forfeit our faith in God.

One of Job's friends put it this way:

> Think about the many people you have taught and the weak hands you have made strong. Your words have comforted those who fell, and you have strengthened those who could not stand. But now trouble comes to you, and you are discouraged; trouble hits you, and you are

terrified. You should have confidence because you respect
God.

—Job 4:3–6

If we are going to get over any offence, we must operate from two sides. One side is forbearance and the other is forgiving.

Forbearance is focusing on ourselves. It has to do with our patience. Even more, forbearance is the ability of a person to exhibit self-control. Forbearance comes from your affection not your emotions. The affection you have toward your spouse (that of love) should override any emotional moment you may encounter.

Forgiving is focusing on others. I always like to say, "Forgiving is for giving not for keeping." When you have the heart to forgive, someone can offend you and your conclusion is like Jesus. Before He died on the cross He said, "Father forgive them; for they know not what they do" (Luke 23:34, KJV). In essence, Jesus did not announce their innocence, He proclaimed their ignorance.

When your spouse does or says something offensive, don't be quick to charge it to their heart. Instead, charge it to their head. Just say, "I forgive them for they know not what they do."

Through the concept of forbearing and forgiving, Job was able to recover from his illness. All his possessions were restored. Many like to say he received double for his trouble. However, I see it differently. I like to say, "Job received trouble for his double!"

In other words, the devil knows your promotion is just beyond the next horizon. He'll do whatever it takes to get you out of place. Many seek a blessing from God. However, God is not looking at the blessing more than your lesson. He uses every trial and storm to develop your character and faith in Him.

In 1949 Jackie Robinson became the first black batting champion and the first black to receive the National League's Most Valuable Player Award. Robinson was the first black to play at any level in the major leagues. Among his many accomplishments, Robinson was the first black to be enshrined in the Baseball Hall of Fame.

Both Jackie Robinson and Job possessed resilient characters. When you have the character of resilience and your faith is placed in God, you can encounter and overcome any difficulty. And just like these great men, when faced with these hurdles of life, you too will be able to get over it!

ASPIRATION

Winning and losing is inevitable; what isn't acceptable is quitting.

Aspire for Higher

ASPIRATION

Chapter Fifteen

The eagle is one of God's most interesting creatures. It is the national bird of this great nation, the United States. While doing some research on the eagle, I discovered some intriguing facts.

Eagles do not sweat. Therefore one of the methods used for cooling themselves is holding their wings away from their bodies. The female eagle is typically larger than her male counterpart. However, eagles that mate have no problems understanding their individual roles in the relationship.

Although eagles don't possess vocal cords, they make sounds that are mainly for mating and protection against predators. They have very keen eyesight. On average, an eagle's eye is almost the size of a human's, but its sharpness is at least four times greater than a person with perfect vision.

The eagle mostly builds its nest among extremely tall trees or in the cleft of high mountains. Its wings are long and broad, making them effective for soaring. Now, here lies the most interesting feature for this particular fowl—soaring. Just about all birds have the ability to fly. However when you think of the eagle, soaring comes to mind. In order to fly, one needs to move through air or before the wind. However, soaring carries the connotation of lifting oneself to a higher elevation; to ascend to a higher or more exalted level.

I've been married for some time now, and I have discovered a fundamental factor for a healthy marriage is the couple's ability to possess the character of aspiration. Aspiration is best described through the life of an eagle. Just as an eagle aspires to soar, the couple must aspire to go higher in life.

Healthy marriages are a result of dreaming bigger, digging deeper, and reaching farther. Your motive causes you to dream bigger.

Motivation fuels you to dig deeper. Your motion is always to reach farther.

Dreaming Bigger as Your Motive

The ability to dream bigger affords us the opportunity to live better. Our greatest failures can come if we focus too much on our last success. Subsequently, your marriage will not survive or thrive with dreams only for the wedding ceremony.

Too many marriages suffer because the couple's vision for the marriage was myopic at best. Remember, the eagle possesses extraordinary eyesight. For that reason, the eagle is able to see well beyond its immediate surroundings. When couples possess the ability to see beyond what is present, their marriage will progress.

When I speak of the motive for your marriage, I am focusing on the *intrinsic* force that compels you to operate. A person's motive is often hidden from plain sight. However, a motive is your reason for action. Our success is largely due to our ability to dream bigger, better, and brighter. In other words, you should never reach a place in your marriage or your life where you settled for less than the best. God gives us dreams so that we may aspire to be better in life.

Consider the following passage:

> God does speak—sometimes one way and sometimes another—even though people may not understand it. He speaks in a dream or a vision of the night when people are in a deep sleep, lying on their beds.
>
> —Job 33:14–15

God spoke to a young man by the name of Joseph. He gave Joseph dreams of one day becoming great. Not everyone was excited about Joseph's dreams. His brothers despised him because he aspired to be elevated in life. You see, Joseph was an eagle, but his brothers were a flock of ducks. Ducks only quack and complain. Eagles, on the other hand, spread their wings and soar.

Ducks do more flapping than flying. This is what Joseph's brothers did. They flapped their lips and complained about their lives, and

Joseph's dreams were a constant reminder of where they settled. Even though an eagle's life isn't easy, an eagle is willing to soar higher and not settle lower.

No matter what the trouble, Joseph was able to rise above it. He soared above his brother's deception, Potiphar's disappointment, and the prison's discouragement. Joseph was a dreamer! When the situation was too small, he dreamed bigger. When circumstances got worse, he dreamed better. When times got dark, he dreamed brighter.

Aspiration causes you to dream when life seems uninteresting. My friend, don't throw in the towel and quit on your marriage because it seems to have lost its life. Ervin "Magic" Johnson once said, "In life, winning and losing is inevitable. However, what isn't acceptable is quitting." What a profound and true statement.

When we allow ourselves to dream, we will always see our present situation not as it is, but as it can be. When you married, hopefully, it was for better and for worse. Oddly enough, sometimes, the better comes after the worse. You must have vision to see through a storm.

What really makes your marriage work is not how perfect you and your spouse are, but how you are able to cope with one another's imperfections. When your motive is right, your marriage will benefit greatly.

DIG DEEPER AS YOUR MOTIVATION

Years ago, I was told cart drivers had a unique way of getting their donkeys to pull carts. They would tie a carrot at the end of a stick and dangle it in front of the donkey, but always out of the donkey's reach. The donkey would go after the carrot while pulling the cart in the process.

Some might say that is a cruel technique, and you would not get any argument from me. In fact, what some consider motivation is really manipulation. Whenever someone uses sex, money, or any device to take advantage over their mate, it is considered manipulation. God does not want us using manipulation in marriage. In contrast, motivation is a fundamental way to keep the marriage healthy.

When I speak of motivation, I am talking about the *extrinsic* factor or force that influence you to do well. When David heard the challenge of the giant Goliath against God's people, he said, "Is there not a cause?" (1 Sam. 17:29, KJV). Against all odds, David was able to overcome his adversary because he had a reason. Your marriage will last with a cause, not "just *because!*"

The cause is another way of saying motivation. When you are motivated you will be driven, not drifting. Those who drift through life or in their marriage have no purpose. Theirs is a life of happenstance. The drifters hope something good occurs. However, the drivers set a course and with motivation expect to reach their destination.

One day I decided to plant a tree in my yard. I dug a hole in the dirt, planted the tree, and provided the necessary water. A week later I noticed the tree losing leaves. It was the middle of April, and I knew something had gone awry. Soon the tree died.

I went back to the store and purchased another tree. Furthermore, I spoke to a sales clerk who boasted about his horticultural skills. I asked questions on the proper way to plant a tree to prevent future slayings. I discovered burying my tree wasn't good enough. Due to the harshness of my soil, I had to dig deeper.

The lesson I learned in my yard can be utilized in marriage. When the soil of your marriage is hard and nice words have withered, don't pull up or pull out—dig in and dig deeper! Your motivation should become the driving force that causes you to take your marriage to a higher level.

In Proverbs 31 there is a couple whose motivation caused their marriage to flourish. The chapter's primary focus is on the wife. Nevertheless, the husband's role is just as significant. The scripture confirms, "Her husband is known at the city meetings where he makes decisions as one of the leaders of the land" (Prov. 31:23).

Correspondingly, the wife's exploits are put on display. The following is a laundry list of her accomplishments:

1. She looks for wool and flax and likes to work with her hands.

2. She is like a trader ship, bringing food from far away.

3. She inspects a field and buys it. With money she earned, she plants a vineyard.

4. She does her work with energy, and her arms are strong.

5. She watches over her family and never wastes her time.

The list truly goes on concerning this wife and mother. One of the rewards to her faithful service is the accolades she receives from her children and the praises given by her husband.

Read the following account from Scripture:

> Her children speak well of her. Her husband also praises her, saying, "There are many fine women, but you are better than all of them."
>
> —PROVERBS 31:28–29

There should be no greater motivation than appreciation from your family. After all, why did you get married? Others may seek to receive The American Mother and Father Medals or recognition from The Annual Stellar Marriage Awards. However, those who possess the character of aspiration, receive reward from seeing their marriage rise to another level.

A man found a cocoon of the emperor moth and took it home to watch it emerge. One day a small opening appeared, and for several hours the moth struggled but couldn't seem to force its body past a certain point.

Deciding something was wrong, the man took scissors and snipped the remaining bit of cocoon. The moth emerged easily, its body large and swollen, the wings small and shriveled.

The man expected the wings to spread out in their natural beauty, but they didn't. Instead of developing into a creature free to fly, the moth spent its life dragging around a swollen body and shriveled wings.

The constricting cocoon and the struggle necessary to pass through the tiny opening was God's way of forcing fluid from the moth's body into the wings. The mercy snip, in reality, was cruel.

In case you are wondering why the struggle, if you are contemplating giving up on your marriage—know God sees what's happening.

The struggle is needed to develop your spiritual wings. Both you and your spouse were created to soar not drag about with a swollen body.

Reach Farther with Your Motion

The hummingbird is unique in that it has this aeronautical ability. Of the entire bird species, the hummingbird is the only bird that can fly backwards.

Some couples are excited they can fly. In other words, having their marriage off the ground is all they desire. Now, I'll admit, getting your marriage off the ground is good, but it's not good enough. Some people wonder why they keep passing the same problems or argue over the same issues with their spouse. The reason is they are flying like the hummingbird. Instead of moving forward, they are moving backward.

Remember, aspiration is not merely flying, it is soaring. There is a motion involved. The motion in your marriage should cause you to reach farther. When you reach farther it shows you won't settle for mediocrity.

The following quote bespeaks a marriage affected by right motion:

> Life has taught us that love does not consist in gazing at each other but in looking outward together in the same direction.
>
> —Antoine de Saint-Exupery[1]

When you and your spouse decide to reach farther, you create a motion for your marriage. This motion causes you both to be on the same page and moving at the same pace.

Whenever the term *reach* is used, it conveys to stretch out, embrace, or to get in touch with someone or something. In light of this, it would do us all good to reach out more. In the beginning of marriage, couples stand and confess their wedding vows. To every question of will you have, hold, etc., the couple affirms with the words, "I do." After the wedding, they have the rest of their lives to figure out what "they did."

In order to discover your spouse more, in order to discover yourself more, you must be willing to reach farther.

One night a good friend and I were coming home from Dallas, Texas. We were in my Dodge Durango at the time. After a long day, I was too tired to drive. Therefore, he offered to take on the task. This was his first time behind the wheel of my truck, and I must admit, he seemed a bit anxious.

After adjusting the mirrors and seat to his liking, he started asking a bunch of questions about the various features of my vehicle. What's this for? How about this? What will happen if I turn this? He hurled one question after another my way. I wasn't too bothered until he asked about two particular buttons beneath my steering wheel.

I wasn't aware of the functions of those particular buttons and told him so. For this reason, his interest peaked. He asked, "Can I push them?" I wasted no time with responding, "No!" "Why not?" he replied. My answered returned just as quick, "'Cause I said so!" I will admit, by now I was frustrated.

Then there was silence. Finally, I took advantage of our peacetime and fell asleep. Not long after, I was awakened by an enthusiastic cry. I looked in my friend's direction, and he said, "I discovered what those buttons are for." I said, "You mean the buttons I asked you not to touch." Then I thought, well, the truck's still moving and nothing is destroyed. So I asked him, "Tell me, the purpose of the buttons?" He informed me of their purpose, and I must say I enjoyed having the knowledge.

In marriage there will invariably come a time when you will push the buttons of your spouse, and they will no doubt push your buttons. There is a normal inclination to protect certain buttons in your life. However, when you and your spouse desire to reach farther; certain buttons must be pushed. This is how you will connect, allowing you to be on the same page and the same pace.

It is possible to purchase a truck like I did and drive it for years and not know all of the truck's capabilities. So it is in marriage, you can be married for years and still not know each other fully. This is why it is important to reach farther. The motion you share and the direction you seek should be in unison with your spouse.

You know there is one more unique quality about the eagle that I must share. Once paired, eagles (bald eagles in particular), remain together for life.

This is a quality that we should aspire to have. Through the character of aspiration, we strive to dream bigger, endeavor to dig deeper, and commit to reaching farther. By this, we aspire to go higher!

THANKFULNESS

An attitude of gratitude for living, learning, and loving.

Say Your Grace

THANKFULNESS

Chapter Sixteen

A man walked into a barbershop looking to get a haircut. The shop was kept extremely neat. There was only one barber and he was standing at an empty chair. The barber motioned for the customer to sit in the available seat.

The man moved with a particular briskness. His face lit with enthusiasm. Intrigued by the man's cheerful disposition; the barber asked, "Why so happy?" The man explained with excitement, "I'm taking a trip to Rome!"

As he began to cut the man's hair, the barber asked, "What airline are you traveling on?" The man responded, "Trans-Air." The barber's face contorted as he replied, "Trans-Air is the worse to take. They lose your luggage. Their flights are always delayed and their seats are very uncomfortable."

Probing further, the barber asked, "What hotel are you staying in? The man with reservations replied, "Saint Marks Hotel." The barber tightened his face as if in pain and said, "Are you kidding me? I heard of all the hotels over there, that one is the shoddiest. The rooms are stuffy. The service is poor. Most of all, you can't get decent channels on their televisions."

As he was just about complete with the man's haircut, the barber asked, "Why are you going to Rome?" By now the man was really bothered by all the barber's pejorative comments. However, to avoid confrontation, the man tersely answered, "I'm going to Vatican City in order to see the Pope." And right on cue, the barber with sarcasm offered, "You won't like the Vatican City this time of year. The weather is awful. The place is packed with tourists. Above all, you will never get a good look at the Pope because he's kept at a great distance from the common people."

Finally, the man's haircut was complete. The man paid the barber and left his shop as fast as he could. In just a short time, the man went from feeling delighted to feeling dejected. The barber followed the man out the door with cynicism and said, "Try to enjoy your trip."

Did you know the deciding factor between a good life and a bad one or an excited marriage versus a dull one depends on a person's attitude? I have discovered the key to fulfillment. To find fulfillment you need not look for pleasures, possessions, or positions. Fulfillment is obtained by being thankful. To many, the previous statement might come off as being clichéd. However, the simple fact is this: thankful people are happy people. Unthankful people are unhappy people and typically try to cause others to be unhappy.

Everyone has reasons to be thankful. No matter your background, no matter your past or present, you have reasons to be thankful. We can all be thankful for living, learning, and loving.

THANKFUL FOR LIVING

Couples who have learned to appreciate life experience far less stress in their marriage. By no stretch of the imagination am I purporting thankfulness brings less trouble. We all will experience trouble. Nevertheless, people who are thankful choose to focus on the positives. Thankful people learn to appreciate both the good and bad times.

Consider the following quote for further understanding:

> Gratitude in its deepest sense means to live life as a gift to be received thankfully. And true gratitude embraces all of life: the good and the bad, the joyful and the painful, the holy and the not-so-holy. We do this because we become aware of God's life, God's presence in the middle of all that happens.
>
> —HENRI NOUWEN[1]

The understanding is simple. We can appreciate life no matter the circumstances because we share the life of our Lord Jesus Christ. Remember, problems you face in your marriage and difficulties in life provoke God's presence. The Lord announced to Moses that He saw the afflictions of His people and knew their sorrows (Exod. 3:7). It would be enough just to know God is acquainted with grief. Better still God says, "I am come down to deliver them" (Exod. 3:8, kjv). Note, God's presence is provoked through our pain.

Therefore, we are left with a life to be celebrated through thanksgiving. God gives us life, not to grudgingly endure but to gratefully enjoy. It's called abundant living. Do the days of your week look like A Sad Sunday, A Mundane Monday, A Tedious Tuesday, A Wearisome Wednesday, A Thankless Thursday, A Frustrating Friday, or A Senseless Saturday? Hopefully your week doesn't resemble a corpse (lifeless). However, if it does, Jesus came to give life to the marriage threatened with death, light to the heart filled with darkness, and love for the person on the verge of destruction.

Listen to Jesus' words of comfort:

> A thief comes to steal and kill and destroy, but I came to give life—*life in all its fullness.*
> —John 10:10, emphasis added

Andrea and I have discovered cherishing the memories of our union is great, but savoring each moment is far better. Life is a gift! To share life with a friend is priceless. As you live each day, never neglect to be thankful for the days you live.

Thankful for Learning

I'm sure you have heard the saying: Everything is not what it seems. What about this one? You can't judge a book by its cover. These idioms remind us that learning is essential.

If you are to enjoy your marriage, you will have to become open to modifications. Those who resist change actually resist learning. Change tends to challenge us. Ultimately, the goal of the child of God is to change into the image of Jesus.

The apostle Paul challenged us with these words:

> So here's what I want you to do, God helping you: Take your everyday, ordinary life—your sleeping, eating, going-to-work, and walking-around life—and place it before

God as an offering. Embracing what God does for you is the best thing you can do for him. Don't become so well-adjusted to your culture that you fit into it without even thinking. Instead, fix your attention on God. *You'll be changed from the inside out.* Readily recognize what he wants from you, and quickly respond to it. Unlike the culture around you, always dragging you down to its level of immaturity, God brings the best out of you, develops well-formed maturity in you.

—ROMANS 12:1–2, THE MESSAGE, EMPHASIS ADDED

If we are going to receive the kind of change God desires for us, we must be willing to learn. I'll go as far as to say we must have a thankful attitude toward learning. Married couples who love to learn encourage one another to succeed. However, when married couples despise learning, their marriages become hum-drum and hard.

A couple was celebrating their sixtieth wedding anniversary. Amazed, someone asked the husband how they were able to stay married for so long. The husband said, "Well, it was easy. In our first year of marriage, my wife and I went horseback riding in the mountains of Colorado.

While on the trail, my wife's horse stumbled and she said, "That's once!" Moments later, the horse stumbled again and she said, "That's twice!" Soon after, the horse stumbled again. She took out a pistol and shot the poor horse. Immediately, I began protesting about her mistreatment of the steed. She looked me in the eyes and said, "That's once!"

There's great benefit in learning your spouse. When you are thankful toward learning, your union will be replete with life's rewards. And your marriage will be conducive for love.

THANKFUL FOR LOVING

The greatest discovery I ever made was the love of God. I devoted my last book, *Marriage Matters: Learning to Love Like God*, to God's love. Even more, it reveals how we must learn to love *like* God. However, before we can love like Him, we must be thankful for His love.

Through the love of God we can love our spouse, children, and others. God's love is uncommon and unusual; but thankfully, it's not unobtainable. Freely God gives His love, and He expects us to freely give it away.

When we have God's kind of love operating in our marriage, we can expect wonderful things to occur. First of all, God's love liberates us. Without His love we are consumed by fear. The Bible says perfect love erases all fear (1 John 4:18). Once we love God, we are released to love others the way God loves us and them—unconditionally. Interestingly, we prove our love for God in the way we love those around us.

Ponder this scripture:

> If people say, "I love God," but hate their brothers or sisters, they are liars. Those who do not love their brothers and sisters, whom they have seen, cannot love God, whom they have never seen. And God gave this command: Those who love God must also love their brothers and sisters.
>
> —1 JOHN 4:20–21

Secondly, being thankful for loving means you appreciate the opportunity to show and share your love. The world is hard enough without us adding bitterness and disappointment to it.

When you love like God, you will incorporate three concepts. You will look, listen, and lift.

LOVING LIKE GOD
Look: seeing people with problems not as problems
Listen: hearing with your heart in order to help
Lift: pulling people forward regardless of their failures

Peter and John were on their way to a prayer meeting when confronted by a crippled man. This man was begging for money in hopes to ameliorate his condition. What happened next was straight from the heart of God.

The Bible says Peter and John looked straight at him (Acts 3:4).

Then they listened as the man begged for money. How often do we avoid looking straight at another's horrible condition? Married couples struggle because they fail to see the pain of their spouse. Peter heard with his heart and was able to detect exactly what the man needed. Communication in marriage should begin with listening not speaking.

The scripture discloses Peter took the man by his right hand and lifted him up. Amazingly, the cripple man walked. So it is with every marriage that loves through looking, listening, and lifting.

Let's return to the man who received a haircut from the negative barber in this chapter's opening story. Three weeks after returning from his trip to Rome, the barber and man ran into each other.

The barber asked with sarcasm, "How was your trip to Rome?" The man responded jubilantly, "The trip was great!" The barber suspiciously asked, "How was the flight going over there?" The man spoke up, "The flight was excellent, with plenty of leg room." The barber probed further, "Well, how about the hotel?" The man responded resoundingly, "The hotel was wonderful and the service superb!"

Finally, the barber skeptically replied, "Well, I know you didn't see the Pope." The man with enthusiasm announced, "Yes! I saw the Pope. I was so close to him, he whispered in my ear." The barber now baffled at what he heard demanded, "Tell me, what did he say?" The man couldn't hold back his smile. He said, "The Pope came close and whispered in my ear—that's the worst haircut I've ever seen."

My friend, when you are not thankful for life, learning, and loving, you will become a negative person. The problem with being pessimistic is that negativity always comes back to you.

The spirit of thankfulness will bring you into God's abundant living.

In life, never forget—say your grace!

FAITH

The far out is never out of sight.

Hold It Together

FAITH

Chapter Seventeen

Andrea and I took our daughters to a big tent circus. Of course our daughters were excited about seeing the various animals. I always enjoy seeing the lion act, and Andrea is partial to clowns. However, there was one portion of the show that put us all on the edge of our seats. We all agreed, the trapeze act was the highlight of the event.

There is something about watching trapeze artists as they execute the balancing, swinging, and hanging with such grace. The audience holds their collective breath as the performers flip and toss effortlessly. I find it quite amazing that they operate 100 feet or more in the air. Even still, the mental concentration it must take to pull off such precise feats is puzzling.

The swinging doubles trapeze act featured two performers working together. One performer operated from the position of the catcher, while the other maintained the role of the flyer. Now it was absolutely imperative that the catcher was strong enough to bear the weight of the flyer. Even more, the flyer had to overcome any doubt and fear in order to maneuver in the air. Above all, the flyer had to believe in the catcher's ability to catch him or the act would not have been successful. As anticipated, the performance was spectacular!

Marriage, much like a trapeze act, requires people to trust each other. Furthermore, the couple will need to establish faith in both the heart and hand of God. Therefore, as I write the final chapter of this book, I think it fitting to cover the character of faith.

> The fundamental fact of existence is that this trust in God, this faith, is the firm foundation under everything that makes life worth living. It's our handle on what we can't

see. The act of faith is what distinguished our ancestors, set them above the crowd.

—HEBREWS 11:1–2, THE MESSAGE

FAITH IS FOR THE FIGHT

Having faith and being faithful are among the greatest characteristics one can possess. Nothing is obtained without faith. It takes faith to have a good marriage. A successful marriage is not found, but rather it's filled with two people working and believing the good outweighs the bad. The bitter is working toward the better—by faith, the *far out* is never *out of sight.*

Understand hardships will come, but only to try your faith. Authentic faith is not to avoid trouble, it is to get you through trouble. Make no mistake, faith is for the fight not flight. In other words, your faith is built to take a stand not flee from the scene.

Many people give up on God because they are facing problems. They feel God has forsaken them. On the contrary, God has given them faith to overcome any trial.

Paul encouraged his young protégé Timothy to "fight the good fight of faith" (1 Tim. 6:12, KJV). This is great advice! When life deals more adversities than advantages, when the only company misery seems to have is you, shake yourself and fight the good fight of faith.

The Bible speaks about four men who were afflicted with leprosy. These men were down, destitute, disappointed, and desperate. Their situation went from bad to worse. They sat outside of a city that was suffering a famine. They had no place to stay and seemingly, no one who cared. However, not falling victim to fate, they declared this statement of faith, "Why do we sit here until we die?" (2 Kings 7:3).

The scripture says as those lepers walked, the Lord made their enemies hear armies and weapons of war. Therefore, the enemy fled with haste leaving behind enough spoils for the lepers and the famished city (vv. 6–7).

God can do the same for you in your marriage, on your job, and with your children. All He requires of you is to believe He can. Two words and how you choose to use them can make the difference between being a victor or a victim.

Read the following two scriptures:

> Yea, they spake against God; they said, *Can God* furnish a table in the wilderness?
> Yea, they turned back and tempted God, and *limited the Holy One of Israel.*
> —PSALM 78:19, 41, KJV, EMPHASIS ADDED

Although God delivered Israel from bondage they continually doubted His ability to sustain them. This is evident because at the first sign of trouble they said, "Can God?" Those two words overshadowed God's power and shaped their predicament. Rather than choosing to ask, "Can God?" Israel could have reversed the two words professing, "God can!"

The challenges we face in marriage don't have to wear us out, not if we know God can! God can do what we are incapable of doing. He can give what we don't have to give. He can go where we cannot go. Strong faith is not just believing God *can* do something and it's not merely believing God *will* do something. Strong faith knows He *has already* accomplished what is needed.

In the fight of life, I have incorporated the following mantra:

> God will not allow my mind to conceive,
> What I physically could not achieve.
> Therefore, if I believe I shall receive. Amen!

FAITH BEYOND FAILURE

I bought a new Blu-ray player for my television. When I returned home with it, I wasted no time. I tore into the box, by-passed the instructions, and proceeded to power up my new toy. Andrea asked if I needed help. I just smiled in her direction as I thought, *Does a bird need help flying or a fish swimming?* Of course I didn't need help. I had everything under control (or so I thought).

When it came time to program and operate the various functions and features of this gadget, it didn't make any sense. I tried reading the instructions, but the writing appeared to be coded language that only a foreign spy could decipher.

After a few hours, I finally conceded to the fact that I had failed. As much as it injured my ego, I decided only one course of action was needed. With my manhood wounded, I called my wife's name, "Andrea—Andrea!" When she appeared, I continued whimpering and whining like a sick pup. "*Help* me fix this machine," and "*How* do you get this cacophony contraption to work?" Okay, maybe I didn't say "cacophony contraption," but it expresses best what I felt at the time, so go with it.

Andrea made an attempt to grab the remote to the Blu-ray player out of my hand, but I pulled away. She made yet another attempt and I persisted to resist. For this reason, Andrea asked, "Tyrone, do you trust me?" "Well, yeah" was the answer I gave. She went on to explain, "If I'm going to fix the problem, you have to give up the remote control." I did, and within minutes Andrea had the machine up and fully operational.

I learned something valuable from that experience. Calling for Andrea's help and asking how it worked was good, but not good enough. It wasn't until I released the controller that I found my answer. Just as I gave the remote to Andrea, we must be willing to give God full control of our lives.

Faith operates correctly when we ask for God's *help*, seek God's *how*, and say, "God, *here*."

THREE STEPS TO FAITH
God, Help: we must call upon the name of the Lord.
God, How: we must seek His instructions for our lives.
God, Here: we must place every situation in His hand.

Never allow your failure to keep you from your God. Unfortunately, many marriages have suffered due to one or both spouses refusing the counsel of God. God loves you, and it is His good pleasure to see you do well.

There is no greater example of having faith beyond failure than the biblical couple Abraham and Sarah. God promised them a child.

After some years had passed, Abraham and Sarah decided they were too old to have children. Not wanting to put God in a bad light, they decided to help Him out. Abraham fathered a child with his wife's much-younger slave. Now, I don't have to tell you things got pretty messy.

Abraham failed when he tried to do things his own way. On the other hand, once he practiced the three steps to faith, he reaped the rewards. When presented with the problem of posterity, Abraham asked for God's help (Gen. 15:2–4); God showed Abraham how He would perform the miracle (18:9–14); Finally, Abraham brought his son to the appointed place in order to say, "God, here" (22:1–12). The results of Abraham's faith cannot be counted. God enlarged Abraham's generation beyond measure. Best of all, Abraham is called a friend of God (James 2:23).

Someone coined faith with the perfect acronym.

Forward Action In Trusting Him

When you have faith, failure will not keep you from moving forward. In fact, our failure amalgamated with our faith in God becomes the opportunity to see God's power performed.

FAITH MUST BE FINAL

A man slipped and fell off a cliff while hiking on a mountaintop. Fortunately, he managed to grab a branch that protruded out of the mountain. While holding on, the man looked down and saw fifty feet of jagged rocks below.

In fear, the man started screaming, "Help! Help! Can anyone hear me? Help me please!" Suddenly, a voice from above came forth. The voice said, "My child, I hear you and will help you." The man asked, "God, is that you?" The voice affirmed, "Yes!" The man asked while quailing, "How are you going to help me?" God said, "I will save you if you have faith in Me."

The horrified man responded, "Yes, Lord, I have faith. Please help me! Just help me!" Then God said, "If you have faith in Me, let go of the branch." The man thought for a quick second, then screamed, "Is there anyone else up there?"

The problem with many of God's children is not the absence of faith; it's holding on to our faith when trouble hits. We need to settle it; our faith must be final. I love what the apostle Paul wrote.

> I have fought a good fight, I have finished my course, *I have kept the faith.*
> —2 TIMOTHY 4:7, KJV, EMPHASIS ADDED

That should be the goal of every Believer—to keep the faith. When I stand before God, I want Him to say I kept my faith. On several accounts Jesus had to do a faith check with His own disciples. Jesus would ask them, "Where is your faith?" (Luke 8:25).

If we are not cognizant, there are a lot of things that can cause us to lose our faith. We can lose our faith because of the death of a loved one. Our faith can become displaced when our money is depleted. Our faith can go up in smoke when our health goes down and out. No doubt these examples can cause questions, but we should never question God. In the time of a crisis, we will either learn more about the God we have faith in or we will lose the faith we say we have in God.

When your marriage appears to be falling apart at the seams, it's through faith you hold it all together. The key is not to have faith in your faith, but rather have faith in your God. A lot of people have faith in their faith. Therefore, if things don't occur according to their liking, they figure their faith doesn't work. However, those who have faith in God understand even when things go awry, God is working on their behalf.

Chapter 11 of the Book of Hebrews records some heroes of faith. I'm sure you have heard of David, Samuel, Noah, and Abel. I know you have no problem remembering patriarchs like Moses and Joseph. When the subject of faith comes up, we remember Abraham. You may even recall matriarchs such as Sarah, Rahab, and Ruth.

However, what about those who had faith but were not named in this notable chapter? The scripture may not mention their names, but it chronicles the remarkable, heart wrenching struggles in which they endured.

Read the following passages:

> Others were tortured and refused to accept their freedom so they could be raised from dead to a better life. Some were laughed at and beaten. Others were put in chains and thrown into prison. They were stoned to death, they were cut in half, and they were killed with swords. Some wore the skins of sheep and goats. They were poor, abused, and treated badly. The world was not good enough for them! They wandered in deserts and mountains, living in caves and holes in the earth. All these people are known for their faith, but none of them received what God had promised.
>
> —HEBREWS 11:35–39

The faith of these saints resounds through the annals of time. Although they had not received the promise of God, it's not that they won't receive the promise. In fact, they will receive what God has for them. Albeit, it will come in God's timing. When our faith is final we trust God's heart and His hand.

When our faith is final it removes all fear. While teaching the local congregation, my father submitted this acronym for fear:

F orgets the power of your God

E nvisions the worse

A ccepts defeat before the fight

R ejects God's way of deliverance

There is no need to fear when we know the Father's love. The Bible says, "God's perfect love drives out fear" (1 John 4:18). To rid our lives of fear, we must have faith in the Father's love.

Remember the swinging doubles trapeze act? The flyer had complete confidence that the catcher would do his job. The flyer always does in the air what God commands us to do in life: "Be still and know that I am God" (Ps. 46:10). As our Catcher, God will never drop us. He is more than capable of carrying us and holding us with His unyielding love.

To fulfill God's desire for our marriages, we must have the character of faith: the kind of faith that's built to fight, the kind of faith that takes us beyond our failures, and the kind of faith that is final.

Final Thought

In ancient times artisans would mark their creations with a personalized symbol. Even today artists of various sorts engrave their work. Their signature is considered their character or mark. It distinguishes their work from others.

If the artist's work is poor, there character is considered inferior. On the other hand, when the work is great the character is highly recognized. Now, understand that the work doesn't make the craftsman, but it's the craftsman who brings value to the work.

Having a good life should be our goal and work. However, the deception can be to pursue everything that is good. There are some things that may seem good but the reality is they are not good for us.

Eve saw the tree and considered it good. However, it wasn't good for her or her husband. Seeking for the good is counterproductive. We must seek for God rather than for good. Not everything that is good is God, but God and all He has to offer is good.

The Master Craftsman declared, "Let us make man in our image, after our likeness" (Gen. 1:26). His mark is His Spirit. God offers us His Spirit to guard and guide us through life.

I discovered if we are to relate well with our spouse, children, or others, we so desperately need God's Spirit. It is His Spirit that awakens us to the necessity of character. Through character our work and world become good.

I pray this book has a profound effect on your life, and may the truths within it cause you to assess how you handle life's challenges. Excellence happens when we work well with others. Therefore, improving our character improves our chances of experiencing excellence.

Life is a portrait, and character is the signature written on the canvas of our lives.

Notes

CHAPTER ONE

1. John Hagee, *God's Two-Minute Warning* (Nashville, TN: J. Countryman, 2000), 8.

CHAPTER FOUR

1. Barbara Johnson, *Stick a Geranium in Your Hat and Be Happy* (Nashville, TN: Thomas Nelson, 2004), 178.

CHAPTER FIVE

1. Phoebe Cary, "Our Heroes," in William J. Bennett, *Virtues of Courage in Adversity* (Nashville, TN: W Publishing Group, 2001).
2. John Wooden quote found at http://www.brainyquote.com/quotes/quotes/j/johnwooden163015.html (accessed July 26, 2012).

CHAPTER TEN

1. Mother Teresa quote found at http://thinkexist.com/quotation/we-cannot-do-great-things-on-this-earth-only/488037.html (accessed July 27, 2012).
2. Ralph Waldo Emerson quote found at http://quotationsbook.com/quote/37629/ (accessed July 27, 2012).

CHAPTER ELEVEN

1. William J. Bennett, *Virtues of Friendship and Loyalty* (Nashville, TN: W Publishing Group, 2001), 136.

CHAPTER TWELVE

1. Harriet Tubman story found at http://ehistory.osu.edu/world/PeopleView.cfm?PID=81 (accessed July 29, 2012).
2. Charles Stanley, *When Tragedy Strikes* (Nashville, TN: Thomas Nelson, 2004), 31.

CHAPTER THIRTEEN

1. Hoover Dam statistics found at http://www.youtube.com/watch?v=n4o8NISa4Hs (accessed August 7, 2012).

2. Plato quote found at http://www.brainyquote.com/quotes/quotes/p/plato121792.html (accessed July 27, 2012).

CHAPTER FOURTEEN

1. Albert Einstein quote found at http://www.quotedb.com/quotes/2575 (accessed July 17, 2012).

CHAPTER FIFTEEN

1. Antoine de Saint-Exupery quote found at http://thinkexist.com/quotation/life_has_taught_us_that_love_does_not_consist_in/174000.html (accessed July 28, 2012).

CHAPTER SIXTEEN

1. Henri Nouwen, *Turn My Mourning into Dancing* (Nashville, TN: W Publishing Group, 2004), 17.

About the Author

Tyrone and his wife, Andrea, have worked in full-time ministry for more than fifteen years. They serve under the tutelage of Bishop Nate Holcomb, the pastor and founder of Christian House of Prayer Ministries, Inc.

With a heart of compassion and desire to impart learning, Tyrone Holcomb lays out the counsel of God with simplistic ease. He masterfully weaves biblical principles with humorous stories and witty phraseology that inspires laughter, while enabling the listener to grasp and apply the truths of God's Word.

His teachings stem from this premise: Our position in Christ supersedes our condition in life; therefore, when we go through difficulties, our inquiry should never be, "How can I get out of this?" but rather, "What does God want me to get out of this?" In other words, for God it's not about the "blessin" but the lesson we learn while going through the process.

This anointed couple senses the call of God to strengthen and solidify today's marriages. With the understanding that marriage is a picture of Christ and the church, Tyrone Holcomb has authored two pragmatic books, *Marriage Matters: For Better or For Worse* and *Marriage Matters: Learning to Love Like God.*

He and Andrea use these resources to conduct marriage seminars and marital counseling. Moreover, their ministry extends beyond marriage, as they travel the country teaching and preaching the whole counsel of God.

Contact the Author

Tyrone Holcomb

PO Box 2542

Harker Heights, TX 76548

E-mail: tholcomb@chop.org

Phone: 254-547-1413

Other Books by the Author

MAKE YOUR MARRIAGE MATTER MORE THAN EVER BEFORE.

Tap into the good life God has provided for marriages. In *Marriage Matters: Learning to Live Like God*, author and minister Tyrone Holcomb shows readers how to apply God's Word to learn to love their spouse in a whole new way, thereby weathering the storms that will inevitably challenge anyone's marriage. Readers will be able to rekindle their love for their spouse through kindness, overcome struggles through patience, develop a "community of unity," and most importantly, strengthen the pillar of trust. By taking the love that God has freely given to believers and administering that same love to their spouses, readers can recapture the mandate for every believer—to love unconditionally. The result will be an unbreakable bond and a marriage steeped in the good life of God.

Order Your Copy Today!

MARRIAGE MATTERS: FOR BETTER OR FOR WORSE

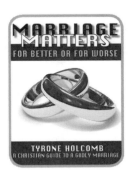

Every married couple and those considering marriage need to know their marriage will experience good and bad times. It's during the bad times that couples begin to question whether their marriage is going to last. Perhaps you are now in that stage of inquiry. Don't give up! Instead, allow God to exhale on your marriage and witness it come to life by every word that proceeds out of the mouth of God. Breath in—breath out—smile, your marriage will live and not die—Marriage Matters.

Order Your Copy Today!